NOTES

ON

NEW TESTAMENT LITERATURE

AND

ECCLESIASTICAL HISTORY.

BY

JOSEPH ADDISON ALEXANDER, D. D.

NEW YORK:
CHARLES SCRIBNER, 124 GRAND STREET.
LONDON: SAMPSON LOW, SON & CO.
1861.

JOHN F. TROW,
PRINTER, STEREOTYPER, AND ELECTROTYPER,
48 & 50 Greene Street.

PREFACE.

THE two fragments presented in this volume, include all that Dr. Alexander left in a condition fit for the press, of his remarkable Biblical and Historical Lectures. It had long been his purpose to write out these Lectures on Old and New Testament History and Literature, but two causes operated to prevent this: First, the pressure of his professional labours, including the preparation of his Commentaries; and secondly, the rapid strides he was constantly making in the knowledge of his subjects, never brought him to the point when he could satisfy his own mind that he was ready to print. It was this fact that gave such vivacity and originality to his instructions, his lectures to each succeeding class being the outpouring of his own acquisitions. These fragments alone remain to us. The brief skeletons of his biblical research, although covering hundreds of pages, could hardly be arranged, and never filled out, by any living man.

I have felt some hesitation in printing beyond § 401, on account of its unfinished condition, but hoping that even these notes may be suggestive to the student of Ecclesiastical History, I concluded to insert them.

S. D. A.

NEW YORK, *Nov.*

CONTENTS.

NEW TESTAMENT LITERATURE.

ECCLESIASTICAL HISTORY.

NEW TESTAMENT LITERATURE.

NEW TESTAMENT LITERATURE.

§ 1. From *lino*, to daub or smear (supine, *litum*), comes *litera*, a mark, and more especially a significant mark—a character—a letter of the alphabet. The plural (*literæ*) denotes—1, the letters of the alphabet collectively—2, then any combination of them in a written composition—whether smaller (e. g. a letter, or epistle, made up of a few letters; or, as we say, "a few *lines*"), or larger (as a book)—3, then books in general, or in the aggregate—and then 4 (subjectively), the knowledge of books ("book-learning"), education—as in Cicero's phrases, "sine literis," "nescire literas," the French "belles-lettres," and the English "man of letters,"

---

§ 1. What is the ultimate root of *literature?* What is the primary and secondary sense of *litera?* What are the idiomatic uses of the plural? What traces of the same in French and English?

meaning much more than a man who "knows his letters."

§ 2. From *litera* itself comes the adjective *literatus*, in form a participle, but without a corresponding verb (as in English), meaning primarily *lettered*, i. e. marked with letters, as a book is lettered by the binder—but secondarily, acquainted with (possessed of) letters, (in the higher sense,) i. e. educated, learned. The plural of this Latin word (*literati*) is still used in English*;* and although the old derivative (*literate*) is obsolete, except in certain technical or legal forms, its previous existence is attested by its opposite, *illiterate*, uneducated, ignorant.

§ 3. From *literatus* (or from *literæ* directly) comes the abstract term, *literatura*, meaning, in the classics, first, alphabetic writing*;* then grammar, philology, the science of *language;* and lastly, learning, education, or the knowledge of books.

As distinguished from *science* in modern parlance, *literature* may be defined as the knowledge of books as books; not merely their contents or

---

§ 2. What is the primary and secondary sense of *literatus?* What traces of this word in English usage?

§ 3. What is the classical usage of *literatura?* What is *literature*, as distinguished from *science?*

substance, but their form, text, language, style, origin, and all that constitutes their [critical and literary] history.

§ 4. The generic term, as thus defined, admits of various specific applications to particular classes or kinds of books, whether differing in form of composition (as poetical and prose literature), or in date (as ancient and modern literature), or in language (as Greek and English literature), or in subject (as medical and historical literature). In this sense every science (or branch of systematic knowledge) may be said to have its "literature;" i. e., a collection of writings peculiar to itself. Thus the modern Germans use the term *Litteratur* to denote the bibliography of any given subject.

§ 5. Among the many possible distinctions and divisions of this nature, one of the most familiar, and at the same time most connected with our present studies, is that of *Sacred and Profane Literature.*

Profane, according to its Latin etymology (*pro*

---

§ 4. How may this generic term be made specific? What relation has literature to the sciences? How do the Germans use the term *litteratur?*

§ 5. What is the correlative or opposite of Sacred Literature? What is the derivation of *Profane?* What is its positive meaning? What is its negative meaning? How may they be exemplified? How is this to be defined?

fano, before the temple, outside of the consecrated precincts), is primarily negative and simply means *not sacred*, though in both languages it soon acquired the positive and stronger sense of irreverent, impious, and even blasphemous. The difference of the primary and secondary meaning may be seen in the equally familiar combinations, " profane history " and " profane swearing." The primary or negative sense must be determined by that of the correlative expression, " sacred."

§ 6. *Sacred Literature* may be taken either in a wider or more restricted application. In the former, it denotes (objectively) the aggregate of books, or (subjectively) the knowledge of such books, on sacred subjects, and is then equivalent to *Religious Literature.* In the latter, it denotes the aggregate (or knowledge) of *sacred writings*, i. e. inspired, and therefore of divine authority; and is then equivalent to *Biblical Literature*, or the literature of the *Bible.*

§ 7. This term (*Bible*) is immediately derived

---

§ 6. What is the twofold sense of Sacred Literature? What is its wider application? What is its narrower application?

§ 7. What is the derivation of *Bible?* What was the primary sense of βίβλος? What was its secondary sense? How is βίβλιον used in the New Testament? How is βίβλος there applied? When was it first applied to the whole Word of God?

from the Latin and Greek plural (*Biblia*), a diminutive of βίβλος (sometimes written βύβλος), which originally means the *papyrus* plant, the inner bark of which was used of old as a material for writing —hence our *paper*, though composed of an entirely different substance. A secondary use of both the English and the Greek word is to signify any piece of writing (as a bill of divorcement, Matt. 19, 7; or a book), in which sense it is applied to the divisions of the Old Testament—the "book of Moses" (Mark 12, 26)—the "book of Psalms" (Luke 20, 42)—the "book of the Prophets" (Acts 7, 42)—but never to the whole of the Old Testament collectively. Its application to the entire Word of God, as the Book of Books, or Book κατ' ἐξοχην, appears to have been introduced by Chrysostom.

§ 8. Another common name for the whole Word of God is *Scripture*, from *scriptura*, *scribo*, corresponding to the Greek γραφή from γράφω, meaning, originally, any writing whether great or small; but applied emphatically sometimes to a single text or passage (as in Luke 4, 21)—sometimes to several in connection (as in Acts 1, 16)—sometimes to

§ 8. What is the derivation of *Scripture*? How is γραφή applied in the New Testament? How is the plural (γραφαί and γράμματα) applied? What epithets are coupled with these plurals? Where does the phrase "Sacred Scriptures" occur?

the whole of the Old Testament (as in John 10, 35. 2 Tim 3, 16)—which is still more frequently denoted by the plural (γραφαί, *scriptures*) of which some find the earliest example in Daniel 9, 2. (Compare John 2, 22 and 5, 39.) With this plural Paul employs the epithets *holy* (Rom. 1, 2) and *sacred* (2 Tim. 3, 15), which are confounded in the English version.

§ 9. The English adjectives derived from these names (*Biblical* and *Scriptural*), although substantially synonymous, are not entirely convertible in usage; the latter being commonly employed to express internal agreement with the Word of God, the former what externally belongs to it, as in the phrases, "scriptural doctrine," "biblical learning," in which the epithets cannot conveniently be interchanged.

§ 10. Applying to the Book which we distinguish from all others as the *Scriptures*, or the *Bible*, the definitions previously laid down, we may understand by the term *Biblical Literature*, in its subjective sense, the knowledge of the Bible, as a book, or of the writings which compose it, as books,

---

§ 9. What is the true distinction (in English usage) between "biblical" and "scriptural"?

§ 10. What is Biblical literature?

not merely of their substance or contents, but of their form, text, language, structure, style and history.

§ 11. Here again, as in the case of Sacred Literature, we may conveniently distinguish a wider and a narrower application of the term; the former comprehending Interpretation, not only as a part, but as the most important part of Biblical Literature, to which its other elements are merely auxiliary.

§ 12. But Interpretation is the business of a lifetime, which, so far from being finished in a course of academical instruction, can only be prepared for and begun. And as this preparation and beginning are not confined to any one department, but diffused, at least in theory, through all, we need a more specific definition of the study upon which we are now entering.

§ 13. *Biblical Literature*, then, in the restricted sense, excludes Interpretation proper, not as being either unimportant or irrelevant, but, on the contrary, as the all-important end to which it is itself a necessary means. In other words, it compre-

§ 11. What is its widest application?
§ 12. Why must interpretation be excluded?
§ 13. What is the more restricted sense of Biblical Literature?

hends those studies which may be regarded as auxiliary to the Exegesis, or the actual Interpretation of the Word of God.

§ 14. *Biblical Literature*, thus defined, may be correctly represented both as an ancient and a modern science. In its essential elements and parts, it is coeval with Interpretation, properly so called. Ever since men have attempted to expound the Scriptures, they have unavoidably made some use of these auxiliary studies; but in ancient times without reducing them to system, as a science or distinct branch of sacred learning. Important contributions, both of material and principle, are due to such men as Jerome and Augustin in the ancient church; to Junilius and Cassiodorus, at a somewhat later date; to Alcuin and Photius in the middle ages. But, as a methodized and systematic science, it is scarcely older than the Reformation, and has been developed chiefly since that great event, especially among the Germans, where it has become a mighty engine for the propagation of sceptical theology, which is a reason not for neglecting it, but rather for its more assiduous culti-

---

§ 14. How old is this science? In what sense is it ancient? In what sense is it modern? When and where has it chiefly flourished? How has it been abused? How is the abuse to be corrected?

vation, as the only antidote to such perversion, and the best security for sound interpretation.

§ 15. Another reason for attending to these studies here is that more than any other they ensure attention to the Word of God hereafter by making it now a subject of investigation as a whole, and in its principal divisions, with their mutual relations, and the most efficient methods of minute and thorough exposition, to be carried out in future life, not as a literary pastime, or a merely intellectual employment, but as the great work of the ministry, by which the staple of its pastoral instructions must be chiefly furnished. This prospective influence on future labor is not so effectually exerted by the minute interpretation of small portions of the Word—however valuable in itself, and in its bearing upon other ends—as by a more discursive and apparently more superficial view of those preliminary and auxiliary studies, which are comprehended in the conventional and somewhat vague term, Biblical Literature.

§ 16. The intimate relation thus existing between these auxiliary studies and the great work of interpre-

---

§ 15. Why should it form a part of theological instruction? In what respect is it more useful than actual interpretation?

§ 16. What was the earliest form given to this science? What

tation led to the early adoption of the Isagogic form and method, which regards them as directly introductory or preliminary (εἰσαγωγη from εἰσάγω, *introduco*) to actual exegesis or interpretation of the Scriptures. Thus the learned Roman Catholic, Pagninus, who died before the middle of the sixteenth century, wrote two works, under the Greek title *Isagoge* (*ad sacras literas*, and *ad mysticos sacræ scripturæ sensus*). The same title was adopted in the next century by the great French Protestant divine Andrew Rivet. (*Isagoge ad Scripturam Sacram*). Carpzovius and others used the corresponding Latin title *Introductio*, which has since become the current one, not only in Latin but in English (*Introduction*) and German (*Einleitung*).

§ 17. The idea of an Introduction, being relative, varied in extent, according to the judgment or convenience of the writer. One of the most comprehensive applications of the title is in Thomas Hartwell Horne's well-known work in four volumes, which embraces all that can be reckoned introductory or even auxiliary to interpretation, not excepting the evidences of revealed religion,

---

was it called in Greek, and by whom? What in Latin? English? German?

§ 17. How much is included in the term introduction? Which part do the Germans commonly exclude?

nor biblical antiquities, geography included, which, though certainly belonging to Biblical Literature in the widest sense, are commonly omitted by the Germans in their technical use and definition of the term Einleitung.

§ 18. The usual practice has been to divide Introduction into two parts: General and Special; the former including what relates to the whole Bible or to one of its great parts, considered as a whole; the other what can be conveniently considered only in connection with the several books.

§ 19. The order of these two parts has not always been the same, though commonly the one first stated. Some writers of celebrity, however, have begun with Special Introduction, for the sake of a more chronological arrangement, by beginning with the history of the several books before reciting that of their collection into one book.

§ 20. This has led in later times to another view of the whole subject and a corresponding difference in arrangement and the mode of treatment, not as introductory to any thing, but as independent

---

§ 18. What has been the usual division of Biblical Introduction?

§ 19. In what two ways have these parts been arranged?

§ 20. What is the historical theory and method? Who introduced the title "Critical History"?

and complete in itself; or rather as a branch of history, literary or ecclesiastical; a theory long ago suggested, although not carried out, by Richard Simon, a learned Roman Catholic, near the close of the seventeenth century, in his *Histoires Critiques*, or Critical Histories of the Old and New Testament, the Versions, Commentators, &c.

§ 21. As this difference affects only the arrangement and the nomenclature of the subject, leaving its substance unchanged, it is purely a question of convenience, or at most of literary taste, which is likely to be variously answered according to the predilection of the writer or the teacher for historical or exegetical studies. There is certainly no ground for the extravagant and vehement denunciation of the older (isagogical) method, by some recent German writers, as unphilosophical and obsolete.* To those who estimate such studies by their bearing on Interpretation, it will always seem more natural to treat them as a branch of it, or rather as an introduction to it; while to others or the same, it will be recommended by its obvious convenience in descending from generals to particu-

* Reuss—Guericke (2d. ed.)

---

§ 21. What is the mutual relation of these methods? What false view has been taken by some recent writers? What are the advantages of the old Isagogical method?

lars, and looking at the Bible as a whole, before examining its parts, at least in the minute details.

22. This subject, even in its most curtailed dimensions, is too vast and various to be subjected to a single process of investigation or compressed into a single course of study and instruction. Of the different divisions which have been proposed or acted on, the most satisfactory in theory and practice is the one founded on the immemorial and universally familiar distinction of the *Old* and *New Testament.*

§ 23. This word, both in English and in Latin (*testamentum*), means a last will, or final disposition of one's property, to take effect after the death of the testator.* It is used in the Latin Vulgate to translate the Greek word διαθήκη, not only when it means a testamentary arrangement (as in Heb. 9, 16. 17), but also when it means a dis-

* It is worthy of remark that while "*testament*" has acquired this secondary meaning, which it would now be folly to disturb, its kindred terms, *testamentary*, *testator*, and *intestate*, are never used in any but their primary and proper application.

---

§ 22. Why must the subject of Biblical Literature be divided? What is the most satisfactory division?

§ 23. What is the origin of "Testament," as thus applied? What is the origin of the phrase "Old Testament"? When was the phrase New Testament applied?

pensation or divine economy (as in Gal. 4, 24. Heb. 9, 15), and when it means a mutual arrangement or a covenant (as in Rom. 11, 27 and passim). From the sense of dispensation or economy the transition was an easy one to that of its appropriate and peculiar revelation, in which sense Paul employs the phrase *παλαία διαθήκη* (2 Cor. 3, 14) in immediate connection with the act of reading (*ἀναγνώσει*,) and with obvious reference to the Hebrew Scriptures. In exact analogy to this apostolical expression, the correlative phrase, *καινὴ διαθήκη*, may be used to designate the Greek Scriptures, or the Christian revelation, though applied in the New Testament itself only to the new covenant or dispensation, of which these books are the written charter or organic law. (See Matt. 26, 28. 2 Cor. 3, 6. Heb. 8, 8. 9, 15. 12, 24.) This analogous use of *καινὴ διαθήκη* is at least as old as Origen, and that of *Novum Testamentum* may be traced still further back, to Tertullian, and perhaps to the oldest Latin version in which this phrase may have coexisted with the kindred one of *Novum Instrumentum*.

§ 24. The distinction here proposed is not con-

---

§ 24. Why may the two Testaments be separately treated? What is the difference in age? In language? In subject?

ventional or arbitrary, but arises from the mutual relation of the parts, which, although constituting one revelation, and inseparable from each other, and reciprocally necessary in the process of interpretation, are still formally so far unlike as to admit and even to require somewhat different exegetical appliances and processes. Such are found necessary in the writings of two different ages, even where the language is essentially the same, as in the case of Homer and Demosthenes, Chaucer and Shakspeare. How much more when the languages are not only different, but of different stocks, as in the case of Greek and Hebrew! The same necessity arises in some measure from the difference of subject and design between a preparatory and completed revelation, a ceremonial and a spiritual dispensation. This division has accordingly been long adopted by the best German writers on the subject.

§ 25. The only plausible objection to the separation here suggested is the one arising from the danger of interpreting the Old and New Testaments without regard to one another; and this is rather theoretical than practical, as all experience shows how utterly impossible that process is, where

§ 25. What objection is there to this method? How may it be answered?

both parts are received as equally inspired. Least of all is such an error to be apprehended either on the part of teachers or of learners, in our public institutions, where the study of both testaments is constantly and simultaneously pursued, as parts of the same uniform and homogeneous system. Where either portion of the Word is neglected for the sake of the other, the abuse must spring from personal obliquity of judgment rather than from any formal distribution or arrangement.

§ 26. If the critical study of the Scriptures were preceded by no early and more superficial knowledge of them; if the Bible were as unknown to the student of theology as the Vedas, or even as the Koran; the only reasonable method would be to dispose of the Old Testament before proceeding to the New. But as we all know something of the Scriptures from our childhood, and the object of professional interpretation is not so much to discover what is new, as to perfect and reduce to system what is partially known already, there is neither theoretical absurdity nor practical inconvenience in pursuing the two studies at the same time in parallel courses. And as most of us are first and best ac-

---

§ 26. Why may the two courses be pursued at once? Why may we begin with the New Testament?

quainted with the later revelation, there is nothing to forbid, if nothing to require or recommend, our taking the last first, and immediately proceeding to the proper subject of this course, to wit: New Testament Literature or Introduction.

§ 27. Applying the previous definitions and distinctions to this part of Scripture, we may understand *New Testament Literature* as denoting the knowledge of the New Testament, as a book, or of the writings which compose it, as books; not merely the truth which they contain, but their peculiar form and literary history.

§ 28. To this as well as to the Old Testament, the same two theories have been applied, with the two corresponding modes of treatment, the Isagogical and the Historical. The former has been commonly adopted till within a few years, Richard Simon's *Histoire Critique du Nouveau Testament* (1689) being rather an apparent than a real exception, and including only a part of the whole subject.

§ 29. The rise of the sceptical theology in Germany was not without effect upon this branch of

---

§ 27. What is New Testament Literature?

§ 28. What two theories and plans have been applied to it?

§ 29. How was it affected by the sceptical theology of Ger-

learning, and was reciprocally aided by it. On the boundary between old doctrines and neology stands John David Michaelis, of Gottingen, whose Introduction to the New Testament was originally published in 1750, carrying out the critical principles of Richard Simon, and doing good service in relation to the text and ancient versions. To the fourth edition of this work were added valuable notes by Herbert Marsh, of Cambridge, afterwards Bishop of Peterboro', translated into German by the younger Rosenmüller (1795). Between the first and fourth editions, Semler had begun to treat the subject rationalistically in his "Apparatus ad libertatem Novi Testamenti Interpretationem" (1767), and his treatise on the free investigation of the Canon (1771—1775). The process thus begun was carried further by Eichhorn, in his Introduction, published during the first quarter of the present century (1804—1827), and reached its height in that of DeWette, the first edition of which appeared in 1826, and the fifth in 1848. In the mean time a reaction had begun, promoted by the learned and ingenious Roman Catholic, John Leonard Hug, whose Introduction appeared first in 1808 (fourth edition, 1847).

---

many? What were the principal New Testament Introductions of this school? Who may be considered as beginning the reaction?

§ 30. Among those who contributed to this reaction was H. F. Guericke, an orthodox and pious Lutheran of Halle, in his Contributions to New Testament Introduction, occasioned by DeWette's publications (1828), his Further Contributions (1831), and finally, his formal Introduction (1843), which may be regarded as a summary of all that went before, designed expressly to resist the infidel tendency of the age, and to maintain the inspiration and divine authority of Holy Scripture. This work was constructed on the old isagogical principle; but in its latest and best form, divided into General and Special Introduction, presenting first what relates to the New Testament collectively, and then what is peculiar to the several books.

§ 31. After this work was printed, but before its publication, another of the same general character was brought out by a young Professor (Reuss) of Strasburg, in which the isagogical method was entirely discarded, and the subject treated, not as introductory to exegesis, but as a branch of history,

---

§ 30. Who continued it? What was the character and plan of Guericke's first edition?

§ 31. What change was introduced by Reuss? What effect had this on Guericke? To what extreme did he go in his last edition? What is the true view of these rival methods? Of what inconsistency was Guericke guilty? (That of retaining the word Isagogik.)

and therefore chronologically ordered, under six successive topics, without any division into General and Special. This arrangement, disapproved by Guericke in the preface to his first edition, was adopted in the second (1853), after having been reissued by its author in a fuller and completer form. Not satisfied with this change, Guericke denounces all adherence to the old isagogical method as behind the age and utterly unscientific; whereas, both arrangements, as we have already seen, are views of the same object from two different points of observation, and the old one has advantages peculiar to itself.

§ 32. As this historical arrangement, although not more scientific than the other, and practically less convenient for our purpose, is ingenious in itself, and likely to remain in vogue until another is discovered, it may not be without use to introduce the scheme, as first proposed by Reuss, and slightly modified by Guericke. The whole subject is reduced to six consecutive heads, without subdivision, and may be expressed as follows:

1. The history of the preparation for the New Testament revelation [or its antecedents].

---

§ 32. Why is it well to be acquainted with the historical arrangement? What are the six topics of Guericke and Reuss?

2. The history of its origin [viz., that of the several books, seriatim].

3. The history of their collection [or of the New Testament Canon].

4. The history of its preservation [or of the New Testament Text].

5. The history of its circulation or diffusion [by the aid of versions].

6. The history of its usage or application * [in the way of exegesis or interpretation].

§ 33. Having thus exhibited the new historical arrangement of the subject, for the purpose of comparison and reference, we now return to the more familiar and convenient isagogical method, which considers the whole subject, not as a chapter of literary history, but as a preparation for the work of actual interpretation, and divides it into two great parts, called *General* and *Special Introduction;* the former, as we have already seen, embracing what relates to the New Testament or all its books, collectively; the latter what belongs to the books singly, and can be satisfactorily treated, only by examining them in detail, and one by one.

* So Reuss (not Guericke).

---

§ 33. What method will be used in this course? What is the primary division of the subject? Why is the extent of general Introduction variable?

The first of these divisions, being rather a conventional or arbitrary than a scientific or a necessary one, may be expanded or contracted at our own discretion.

§ 34. But whatever be the topics comprehended under General Introduction, it is highly important to arrange them, not at random, or by any arbitrary method, such as the alphabetical, but on some rational intelligible principle, by which is not meant one that is purely philosophical or scientific, but simply one for which a reason can be given, as opposed to one that is merely accidental or capricious. The best mode of obtaining such a method in the present case is by adhering to the isagogic principle, considering interpretation as the end to be attained, and then inquiring what preliminary questions must be answered, or may be answered with advantage, before entering on the ultimate and main work of exegesis or actual interpretation.

§ 35. Taking the widest view of General Introduction that has been proposed by any writer, and supposing the interpreter to be incited, not by

---

§ 34. How should its topics be arranged? What is meant by a rational method? To what is it opposed? How may such a method be obtained?

§ 35. What is to be assumed in the application of this principle? What then is the first preliminary question? What other

mere literary curiosity, or vague desire of knowledge for its own sake, but by religious motives, and especially an earnest wish to know the will of God, the first preliminary question which might be expected to present itself is this: What reason is there to believe a revelation possible or necessary—or, if this be granted, what reason is there to believe this book to be the Word of God—or this New Testament to be a part of such a revelation? Supposing this to be determined, the next questions would be: What are the writings which compose this volume? What detailed compositions have a right to a place in this collection? These two questions may appear to involve each other; but the fact is certain that even where the inspiration of the Bible, as a whole, is granted, there may be a doubt as to the parts of which it is composed.

§ 36. A third preliminary question, in the case supposed, is, whether this book, or these writings which compose it, are precisely as they were at first, and exhibit the ipsissima verba of the sacred

---

question does it raise? What is the next question? What other question does it raise? Why do these questions not involve each other?

§ 36. What is a third preliminary question? What other question does it raise? What do these questions presuppose? What is the previous question thus suggested?

writers; or if not, whether they can be restored to their original condition. The solution, and even the investigation, of this question, presupposes some acquaintance with the language in which the book is written. It may, therefore, be presented as a previous or intermediate question, What that language is—its origin—its history—its character—the means by which it may be mastered—and the sources from which illustrations may be drawn?

§ 37. Supposing this essential knowledge to have been acquired, the question in relation to the text may be successfully pursued. But even when it has been answered, it is found that the book, although verbally intelligible, is obscured by perpetual allusions to remote times and places, to peculiar climates, soils, and products, to a state of society unlike our own, to personal habits, to domestic, social, civil, and religious institutions, of a kind with which the reader has no personal acquaintance, and of which he must know something, in a general way at least, before he can attempt interpretation in detail, with any prospect of success. We may now suppose him to have gained this knowledge; but before he enters on the work of exegesis with entire satisfaction, he will naturally ask another question, really including two.

---

§ 37. What is the fourth preliminary question?

§ 38. This is the question: How—upon what principles, the work is to be carried on? How far must the interpretation of this book as an inspired one, be different from that of a mere human composition? And a man of due humility and self-distrust would scarcely fail to add the question, What have others done before me in the effort to explain this book to others, or to understand it for themselves? What rules have they adopted or laid down? and what are the results? What means of illustration, and facilities for study, have they left to their successors? And how may we avail ourselves of their assistance to the most advantage? These concluding questions being satisfactorily answered, the way to a correct interpretation of this part of Scripture is completely open, and requires only to be diligently walked in.

§ 39. This may seem to place the business of interpretation at too great a distance, and to hinder the approach to it by too many obstructions. But this discouraging impression may be rectified by recollecting that it is not the minute detail, in-

---

§ 38. What is the fifth preliminary question? What is the sixth?

§ 39. What objection may be made to the foregoing statement? How may it be answered? What use may be now made of these questions?

cluded under these successive topics, that is absolutely necessary as an introduction to the actual processes of exegesis, but only a correct acquaintance with the main points upon which the rest depend. When these are mastered, even in their principles or outlines, the very process of interpretation will throw light upon the others, and receive light from them by a mutual reflection. But interpretation cannot even be begun, in an intelligent and profitable manner, without a previous solution, however general and superficial, of the questions which have been successively propounded, and the answers to which comprehend the whole of General Introduction in its widest sense. As an aid to the memory, let us briefly recapitulate the questions, and observe their correspondence with the parts of Introduction.

§ 40. To the first question—(what reason have we to regard the Bible as the Word of God?)—the answer is afforded by that part of Introduction, in the widest application of the term, which the Germans call *Apologetik*, and which we, for want of any technical expression, call the *Evidences of Revealed*

§ 40. How is the first question to be answered? How is the second to be answered? How is the third to be answered? How is the fourth to be answered? What is the technical use of the terms "text" and "criticism"?

Religion. To the second question—(what particular writings are entitled to a place in this inspired collection?)—the answer includes all that relates to what is technically called the *Canon of* [*Scripture* or *of*] *the New Testament.* To the third question —(what is the original language, its affinities, its history, its character, the means of its elucidation?) —the answer is afforded by that part of Introduction called *New Testament* [or *Biblical*] *Philology.* To the fourth question—(how may the exact words of the sacred writers be determined? and how far has this been done already?)—the answer is afforded by *New Testament* [or *Biblical*] *Criticism*, i. e. of the *text*, using both words in their technical and narrow sense.

§ 41. The fifth question—(what were the peculiar circumstances of the people mentioned in the Bible, as to country, climate, habits, institutions, some knowledge of which is necessary to a correct determination of its meaning?)—opens the whole subject of *Antiquities* or *Archæology*, including the *Geography* of Scripture. The answer to the sixth question—(what are the principles and laws of

---

§ 41. How is the fifth question to be answered? How is the sixth question to be answered? How is the seventh question to be answered? Why may the sixth and seventh be transposed?

biblical interpretation?)—corresponds to what is technically known as *Hermeneutics*, differing from *Exegesis*, as the science from the art, or theory from practice. But as this is an inductive science, resting more upon experience and common sense than on any abstract speculations *a priori*, it is not to be severed from the seventh and last question—(what has been already done in this department?) —corresponding to the *History of Interpretation*. Indeed, it may be found most convenient in practice, to give this the preference in order of consideration, so as to secure the advantage of historical induction in determining our rules and principles of exegesis.

§ 42. Such is a brief view of the topics comprehended in the widest application of the technical term *Introduction*, and actually treated in some works upon the subject, as for instance that of Horne already mentioned (§ 17). But in order to reduce the field to manageable compass [as well as to accommodate our own arrangements], it will be necessary to eliminate several of these topics, although not precisely on the same grounds. One of

---

§ 42. Where is this scheme carried out in its full extent? Why must it be reduced to narrower limits? How may this be effected? Why may the evidences be omitted? Why may Antiquities and Geography be omitted? Why may Hermeneutics be omitted?

these, the first in our enumeration, though a fundamental and preliminary question, belongs rather to Theology than to Introduction, and is either presupposed or included in that study. Another, holding the fifth place, may be excluded on the ground that it is rather a collateral auxiliary than an introductory preliminary study. This, with its vast extent and growing interest, requires it to be separately treated [as I hope it will be in our course of study]. The only other topic which can be omitted is that of *Hermeneutics*, on the ground that it cannot well be separately handled in connection with the two great divisions of the Bible, but must be disposed of once for all, without regard to this conventional distinction.

§ 43. The elimination of these topics leaves us four, to constitute the first part of our present course, distinguished from the last part by the name of *General Introduction*. I. The *New Testament Canon* (or the books entitled to a place in the collection). II. The *New Testament Philology* (or all that relates to the Original Language). III. The *New Testament Text* and *Textual Criticism* (by which we determine the ipsissima verba of the

---

§ 43. How many topics still remain? What is the first? What is the second? What is the third? What is the fourth? What part of it belongs to Special Introduction?

sacred writers). IV. The *Exegetical History of the New Testament* (including that of Versions, ancient and modern, and that of schools and systems of interpretation, but excluding that of individual books and writers, which belongs to *Special Introduction.*)

§ 44. The transition or connecting link between General and Special Introduction will be furnished by a topic which belongs exclusively to neither, and yet partially to both—to the second, as concerning the particular books—to the first, as necessarily preceding their minute examination one by one. This is the topic of *Classification and Arrangement*, under which we may arrange some matters commonly connected with the Canon, such as the circumstances out of which the Christian Revelation (or New Testament) arose, and the traces of an actual collection of the books into a volume; the canonical history of each book, as detailed proof of its canonicity, belonging necessarily to *Special Introduction.*

§ 45. The first division, then, of General In-

---

§ 44. What is the transition or connecting link with Special Introduction? How far does it belong to both? What may be conveniently referred to this intermediate topic?

§ 45. What is the first topic of General Introduction? What are the questions which it undertakes to answer? Why are these

TRODUCTION is the *Canon of Scripture*, or, according to the distribution which we have adopted (§ 22—26), that of the *New Testament*. By means of the arrangement just proposed (§ 44) we are enabled to reduce this topic to a reasonable compass, introducing only what is absolutely necessary as a preliminary to the others; and in answer to the question, What shall we interpret? answer, the New Testament. But what is the New Testament? What volume is entitled to the name? The Book of Mormon, or the Koran, might be lettered the "New Testament," but this would not entitle them to be so reckoned; and even when we have identified the volume as a whole, the question still remains to be decided, What books are entitled to a place in this collection? Are the twenty-seven books which now compose it those which were acknowledged by the church from the beginning—neither more nor less? The question with which we are directly here concerned is not whether these books are inspired, but whether they were so considered by the church from the days of the apostles, and thereby entitled to a place in the Canon?

§ 46. The Greek word (κανών) may be traced to

---

necessary as preliminary questions? How is this topic related to that of inspiration?

§ 46. What is the etymology of *canon* and *canonical?* What

one originally meaning a *cane* or *reed*—then any straight rod suitable for measuring or for keeping other things straight—with specific application to the beam of a balance—or, as some say, to its perpendicular support—but certainly denoting, as a secondary meaning, any rule or standard, physical or moral. It is then applied, by way of eminence, to the Rule of Faith and to the Scriptures, or inspired Word of God, as constituting that rule.* The sense of *list* or *catalogue* attached by some to this word, is entirely derivative and later in its origin. The cognate adjective to *canon* is *canonical*, belonging to the Canon, or the Rule of Faith. Its correlatives and opposites, *apocrypha*, *apocryphal*, derived from ἀποκρύπτω, to hide from or to hide away, and variously used by ancient writers to denote what is secret or mysterious, anonymous or of uncertain origin, spurious or counterfeit, untrue or fabulous, heretical or doctrinally false, but as a technical and ecclesiastical expression meaning sim-

* "By the straight we judge both itself and the crooked, for the rule is singly the test of both (κριτὴς αμφοῖν ὁ κανών)." Aristotle de Animâ, c. 5, § 16, ed. Trendelenburg, quoted by Archer Butler, vol. ii. p. 385 (ed. W. H. Thompson).

---

is that of apocrypha? What are the various senses of *apocryphal?* What is its technical and strict sense? Why are the Apostolic Fathers not Apocryphal?

ply and specifically something which purports or claims to be a part of Holy Scripture, but is not so, perhaps with the accessory notion of uncertain origin, by which the so-called Apostolic Fathers are exempted from the application of the term, though some of them were anciently regarded as inspired, and their writings read in public worship.

§ 47. The precise point to be determined under this head is the identity of the book which we call the New Testament, and of the writings which compose it now, with those acknowledged, under the same names, from the beginning, as belonging to the Canon or the Rule of Faith. There are two methods of conducting this inquiry, which may be distinguished as the *a priori* and *a posteriori* process. The first consists of a historical deduction in the order of time, tracing the origin of each book, and of the entire collection, with the proofs of their continued existence to the present time. This is the course adopted by those writers who prefer the Historical arrangement to the Isagogical (§ 21, 22, 23). Under the latter plan which we are now pursuing, this deduction may be most conveniently presented in its outlines at the close of the General

---

§ 47. What is the precise point to be settled? What are the two methods of proceeding? What is the *a priori* method? Where does it properly belong? What is the *a posteriori* method?

Introduction in connection with the subject of Classification and Arrangement, and in its details in the Special Introduction to the several books of the New Testament. In this place, and in answer to the preliminary question just propounded, it will only be necessary to present in brief the *a posteriori* argument for the identity of our New Testament with that which came from the Apostles, setting out from undisputed and notorious facts belonging to the present, and then tracing up the testimony to the very times of the Apostles.

§ 48. The fact from which we set out in this *a posteriori* process is the palpable and certain one, that the book now called the New Testament is the same in every language, and throughout the world. This statement has no reference to minute variations of the text, which will be afterwards considered, but to the collection as a whole, and to the smaller books of which it is composed. This uniformity is the more remarkable, because it has no existence in the case of the Old Testament, one of the points of difference between most Protestants and the Church of Rome, relating to the canon of the Hebrew Scriptures; whereas, although the

---

§ 48. What is the starting point in this inquiry? How is this statement to be understood? Is it equally true of the Old Testament?

New Testament apocrypha are still more numerous, not one of them is anywhere regarded as belonging to the Canon, but all critics and all nations and all churches, are agreed in acknowledging the same New Testament, composed of the same twenty-seven books, neither more nor less.

§ 49. The next fact, equally notorious and certain, although more remote from our immediate sphere of observation, is that this identity or uniformity has constantly existed for a period of more than 1400 years; before as well as since the Reformation; through the Middle Ages; back to the close of the fourth century. The evidence of this fact is both negative and positive, arising from the absence of all contrary appearances throughout this series of ages, and confirmed by explicit testimony, at the date referred to, that the same New Testament which we possess, and made up of the same books, was then both in public use and private circulation. This explicit testimony is afforded both by individuals and by collective bodies, of great eminence, and highly qualified to testify without mistake or partiality.

§ 50. In order to preclude all misconception as

---

§ 49. What is the next fact? What is the twofold proof of it? What is the negative proof? What is the positive proof?

to this point, it is proper to observe and bear in mind, that we appeal to fathers and to councils, not as judges, as the Church of Rome does, but as witnesses to matters of fact, of which they were personally cognizant, as well as *ex officio*. The weight of the testimony is to be determined, as in other cases, by the character and standing of the witness as known *aliunde*, by his opportunities of information, and his freedom from all motives to misrepresent. Measured by this rule, one man may deserve more credit than the largest council; but in general the testimony of such bodies is peculiarly important, as embodying the testimony of great numbers; as preceded often by inquiry and discussion; as expressed, not hastily and loosely, but with more or less precision and formality; and, lastly, as transmitted to us, not by vague tradition, but in solemn, and official acts.

§ 51. The fact already stated, that the Canon of the New Testament, at the close of the fourth century, was perfectly identical with that in universal

§ 50. What is the authority ascribed in this argument to fathers and councils? How is their testimony to be valued? What gives peculiar weight to that of councils?

§ 51. What is the testimony of Rufinus? Upon whose authority does it rest? What distinction does he make between canonical and other books? What does he say of the New Testament Apocrypha.

use at present, is attested by *Rufinus*, an eminent Father of the Latin Church, who enumerates the books by classes, namely, the Four Gospels, the Acts of the Apostles, fourteen epistles of Paul, two of Peter, one of James, one of Jude, three of John, and the Revelation of the same Apostle. That this is no subjective judgment of his own, as to what books ought to be received on their own merits, but his simple testimony to a historical fact, appears from his adding to the list, "hæc sunt quæ patres inter canonem concluserunt," using the word *canon* just as we do, and describing it as closed or completed, not by him or his contemporaries, but by the *patres*, meaning, no doubt, those of the primitive or apostolic age. That he does not understand by canonical (as Semler did) such books as were used in public worship, appears from his enumerating others which he calls *ecclesiastici*, and not *canonici*, because the fathers willed them to be read in Church, but not to be adduced in proof of doctrine (such as the Shepherd of Hermas, and Old Testament Apocrypha), and then distinguishes from both classes the New Testament Apocrypha, "quæ legi noluerunt." The same facts are abundantly attested by the still more eminent contemporaries, Jerome and Augustin.

§ 52. This individual testimony, which would

be almost conclusive by itself, is confirmed as to the most essential point, by two contemporary councils, both held in North Africa, then one of the most prosperous and enlightened portions of the Church, within the last ten years of the fourth century. The Council of Hippo (A. D. 393), after ordering that nothing shall be read in church, under the name of Divine Scriptures, " præter Scripturas canonicas," proceeds to specify them in the most deliberate and formal manner: " Sunt autem canonicæ scripturæ evangeliorum libri quatuor,"—then follows one book of Acts, 13 epistles of Paul, " ejusdem ad Hebræos una,"—2 of Peter, 3 of John, 1 of James, 1 of Jude, and the Apocalypse of John, just the Canon of Rufinus, and our own. To this decree it is added: " de confirmando isto canone transmauna ecclesia consulatur "—and accordingly we find it confirmed, not only by a council at Carthage four years later (A. D. 397), but soon after by the bishop of Rome (Innocent I.), and long after by a Roman council (A. D. 494), showing that no change had taken place within a century, as none has taken place within the fourteen centuries that follow.

---

§ 52. How is his testimony confirmed? What is that of the Council of Hippo? By what other witnesses is it confirmed?

§ 53. Going further back in the fourth century, we find among the writings of Athanasius, the most eminent Greek Father of that age, and the champion of the Nicene faith against the Arians, a list of the canonical books of the New Testament, comprising the 4 Gospels, Acts, 7 Catholic epistles, 14 of Paul, and the book of Revelation, as to which last it is added, that it was received as John's by the ancient saints (or holy) and inspired Fathers. This, although in favor of the book, implies that some held a different opinion, and is the first intimation that we come to in this retrograde inquiry, of the least dissent from the existing canon, which was then received not only in the Greek and Latin, but the Syrian Church, as we learn from the fact that Ephrem Syrus, its greatest representative, who died A. D. 378, quotes in his extant writings every one of our twenty-seven books.

§ 54. A contemporary Father of great eminence, Gregory of Nazianzen, says of the Apocalypse that some receive it (εγκρινουσιν), but that

§ 53. What is the testimony of Athanasius, or a contemporary writer? What intimation does he give with respect to the Apocalypse? By what distinct branches of the Church was our canon then received?

§ 54. What does Gregory of Nazianzen say of the Apocalypse? What is the canon of Cyril of Jerusalem? What is that of the Council of Laodicea? Why is its genuineness not essential?

the majority pronounce it spurious (*οἱ πλειους νοθον λεγουσι*). Another, equally distinguished, Cyril of Jerusalem, omits it in his catalogue (including the 4 Gospels, with a positive exclusion of all others, as *ψευδεπιγραφα και βλαβερα*, Acts of 12 Apostles, 7 Catholic epistles of James, Peter, John, and Jude —14 epistles of Paul), then adds: *ΤΑΔΟΙΠΑΠΑ-ΝΤΑΕΞΩ ΚΕΙΣΘΩΕΝΔΕΥΤΕΡΩΙ.* Precisely the same canon is contained in a decree of the Council of Laodicea (360—364), which some reject as spurious, but which certainly belongs to the fourth century, and if not the testimony of a council, is at least that of another (although an unknown) individual.

§ 55. When we reach the early part of the fourth century we come to the famous canon of Eusebius, bishop of Cesarea, the confidential friend of Constantine the Great, and "Father of Church history." He divides the Christian books of his day into three great classes: I. *Homologumena*, acknowledged, undisputed. II. *Antilegomena*, assailed or called in question. III. *Notha*, or (*atopa kai dyssebe*).

---

§ 55. What was the canon of Eusebius? What books does he refer to the several classes? What doubtful position does he give to the Apocalypse? How does he name the classes elsewhere? Why does he place the Apocalypse in the first and third divisions? How is it judged by Dionysius of Alexandria—and why?

Under the first head he enumerates the Four Gospels, Acts, Epistles of Paul (without name or number), 1 John, 1 Peter, and Apocalypse, *εἴγε, φανείη*. Under the third head he enumerates several gospels and acts of the apostles, now universally rejected as apocryphal, with the Book of Revelation, as before, *εἰ φανείη*. Between these, under the title of Antilegomena, he names the five smaller Catholic epistles, with the Acts of Paul and the Shepherd of Hermas. The last two have been universally rejected, and the other five as universally received, since the close of the fourth century, as we have seen. In another place, Eusebius calls the first class *Sacred Scriptures*, represents the second as objected to, but read in most churches, and describes the third as "spurious, and alien from apostolical orthodoxy." In a third place he mentions seven Catholic epistles. He nowhere expresses any doubt of his own, even as to the Apocalypse or Antilegomena, but only records that of others. His placing the Apocalypse in the first or third class, not the second, seems to imply that if not the work of an apostle, it was an "absurd and impious" forgery. Towards the close of the third century, we find Dionysius of Alexandria admitting the Apocalypse to be inspired, but denying the authorship of John, entirely from internal evidence.

§ 56. A little earlier, Origen, the master of this Dionysius, and the most distinguished Father of that age, includes the Book of Revelation in a list of the canonical books, and names John as its author, but omits the five shorter Catholic epistles, and describes that to the Hebrews as containing Paul's thoughts in the language of another. He elsewhere mentions that of James as current (*φερομένη*) under that name, and 2 Peter, 2 and 3 John, as doubted by others—and he once speaks of Peter's two epistles, and of John's in the plural number, and refers to those of James and Jude. His voluminous writings, some of which are lost, are said to contain abundant quotations from all the books now in the Canon. This may serve to show that mere omissions in these ancient catalogues must not be made to prove too much.

§ 57. Cyprian, Origen's contemporary in the Western Church, refers to all the books now in the Canon, except Hebrews, James, 2 Peter, 2 and 3 John, and Jude. Clement of Alexandria, Origen's predecessor and preceptor (A. D. 220), rec-

---

§ 56. What is the canon of Origen? How does he vary from it elsewhere? What parts of the New Testament are quoted in his writings? What may be inferred from this?

§ 57. What is the Canon of Cyprian? What is that of Clemens Alexandrinus? What is that of Irenæus?

ognizes the four Gospels, Acts, 13 Epistles of Paul, 1 of Peter, 1 of John, 1 of Jude, and the Book of Revelation. Hebrews he supposes to have been originally written by Paul, and translated into Greek by Luke. The same writer comments upon 2 John, and alludes to James and 2 Peter, without naming them. His contemporary, Tertullian, the oldest of the Latin Fathers (A. D. 222), mentions all the books except 2 Peter, 2 and 3 John, but represents Hebrews, though canonical, as the work of Barnabas. Irenæus, a connecting link between the second and third century, and also between the Eastern and the Western Church, does not mention 3 John, alludes to James and 2 Peter, without naming them, regards Hebrews as canonical, but not of Pauline origin, and recognizes all the other books as we do.

§ 58. The Muratori Canon, a fragment found at Rome in the 18th century, contains a list of the books read in churches in the time of Pius I., who was bishop of Rome during the second century, omitting James, and leaving 2 Peter doubtful, and giving Hebrews a different name, and not assigning it a place with Paul's epistles. The Peshito

§ 58. What is the Muratori Canon? What is the Peshito? What books of the New Testament does it omit? What lines of testimony here converge?

or old Syriac version, made near the close of the second century, or early in the third, omits 2 Peter, 2 and 3 John, Jude, and Revelation, all which are found in a few manuscripts, but probably of later date.* As to most of the books, we have thus concurrent testimony, at the end of the third century, from Gaul, Asia Minor, Egypt, Italy, and Carthage.

§ 59. Beyond this point we have no formal catalogues, but only references and quotations, the paucity of which may be accounted for by the paucity of writings which contain them; by the slow communication in the ancient world, which caused some writings to be late in gaining general circulation; and by the authority which still belonged to oral tradition, making reference less necessary, even to books which were acknowledged as inspired, and therefore as canonical. But the aggregate testimony of the first and second centuries is amply sufficient to establish the reception of the Gospels, Acts, 13 epistles of Paul, that to the Hebrews, though not always under his name, 1 Peter, 1 John, and the Book of Revelation.

---

§ 59. What is the nature of the testimony beyond this point? How may the paucity of references be accounted for? What is the sum of the testimonies of the first two centuries? What is the result of the whole induction?

Of the remaining books, the one most frequently alluded to is Jude, then 2 John, then James, then 3 John, and then 2 Peter, which is not expressly quoted in the first or second century, though mentioned near its close by Irenæus and Clement of Alexandria. The result of this induction may be therefore summarily stated thus, that 20 of the books now included in the Canon have been homologumena, or undisputed ab initio; while the other seven are less frequently referred to in the early ages, and afterwards spoken of as antilegomena, though universally received into the Canon at the close of the fourth century.

§ 60. The question now is, not whether these seven books shall be received to an inferior place in the Canon, as proposed by Augustine and some of the Reformers, but rejected even by the Council of Trent; but whether they are entitled to a position of perfect equality with all the rest. The obvious reason is, because there can be no such thing as half-canonical or half-inspired; a writing must be

---

§ 60. Why can there not be a secondary canon? What is the true state of the question as to the antilegomena? What is the natural presumption? Where is the onus probandi? What charge is brought against the ancient church? How far is it well founded? How may it be disproved in this case? What absurd assumption would be otherwise required?

either wholly so or not at all. Nor is the question, why should we receive these books, as they were certainly received at the close of the fourth century; but why should we reject them. The presumption raised by their reception then, perhaps on evidence no longer in existence, throws the burden of proof on those who would exclude them. Nor is this presumption weakened by the charge of uncritical negligence, which some allege against the ancient church, a charge not wholly groundless with respect to the text, but shown to be so with respect to the Canon, by the very doubts and difficulties now in question; unless we absurdly assume that the caution previously exercised was suddenly abandoned at the close of the fourth century.

§ 61. The only question which remains is, whether the acknowledged doubts and hesitations as to these seven books can be accounted for on grounds consistent with their having been canonical from the beginning. It is not required that the proof be as clear and as abundant as it is in the case of the other books, but only that it be sufficient to remove all reasonable doubt upon the sub-

---

§ 61. What is the remaining question? What is and what is not required as to the evidence? How far (or in what case) are we bound to acquiesce in the decision of the church at the close of the fourth century?

ject, and confirm the strong presumption which arises from the fact that at the close of the fourth century, the balance, which had oscillated for a course of ages, was unanimously held to preponderate in favour of the books in question. This decision we are not only authorized, but bound, to acquiesce in, as the church has acquiesced in it for fourteen hundred years, provided we can find any probable solution of the question why these books, if canonical, were ever called in question.

§ 62. The sufficiency of such an explanation will not be impaired, but rather strengthened, by its not being uniform or perfectly identical in reference to all the books in question. Such a sameness might indeed be suspicious, or indicative of concert or contrivance for the purpose of securing their admission to the Canon. On the other hand, if all, or nearly all, admit of different solutions, resting upon different circumstances in the origin and history, or in their character and contents, there will be no ground for the suspicion above mentioned, nor for any further hesitation in accepting the unanimous testimony of all Christian writers at the close of the fourth century, that these books

---

§ 62. Why is perfect uniformity of explanation neither necessary nor desirable? What is now to be shown—and how?

were entitled to an absolute equality in this respect, with all the others, as having been canonical from the beginning. That there is varied yet harmonious solution in the case of all these books, we now proceed to show, going only so far into the details as may be necessary for this purpose, and reserving all the rest for other and more suitable occasions. (See above, §§ 44, 45).

§ 63. With respect to the Epistle to the Hebrews, the peculiar and decisive fact is, that the ancient doubts had no relation to its canonicity, but only to its authorship, which is not an essential circumstance, since many books of Scripture are anonymous, and the authorship of some entirely uncertain. That some should have doubted whether Paul, whose name appears in all his other writings, would omit it in this one, was natural enough, especially before men had considered any of the possible solutions of this singular departure from his otherwise invariable practice, such, for example, singling one out of many, as that when the Apostle of the Gentiles found it necessary to address the

---

§ 63. What were the ancient doubts respecting the Epistle to the Hebrews? How may they be accounted for? How may the omission of the author's name be accounted for? How far is this assumption necessary? Why would this epistle be longer than the rest in becoming generally known?

Hebrew Christians, he omitted that official description of himself which adds so much to his authority when writing to the Gentile churches. It is not necessary to affirm that this was really the reason, but only that it may be thus and otherwise accounted for, and also that the class of readers obviously addressed in this epistle would of course prevent its being known so early or diffused so widely as those which bore the author's name, and were addressed to Gentile churches or believers.

§ 64. The Epistle of James is not anonymous, but bears a name of doubtful application, having been really ascribed to three different persons so called, namely, James the Son of Zebedee, James the Son of Alpheus, and James the Brother of the Lord, whom many still believe to be distinct from both the others. This uncertainty might be sufficient of itself to cause some hesitation, which would be of course increased by the erroneous impression, current in all ages, of a doctrinal diversity between James and Paul as to the cardinal doctrine of justification. If such an one as Martin Luther, in his zeal for that articulus stantis et codeatis ecclesiæ, could rashly for a time expunge this epistle from

§ 64. What was the first ground of hesitation as to the epistle of James? What was another more important ground? How did it operate in later times? Why is it now without force?

the Canon, surely the same mistake might generate some doubt and hesitation in the ancient church, although it was canonical from the beginning.

§ 65. Of the four smaller writings, Jude and 2 Peter, 2 and 3 John, it may be observed in general that they are all comparatively short and therefore furnish relatively little matter for quotation, which accounts for the paucity of references to them by the early Christian writers, a fact no more decisive of their being uncanonical than the same fact proves the same thing of the shortest of Paul's writings (the epistle to Philemon) which has never been disputed. Of Jude and 2 Peter in particular, it may be further said that one cause of suspicion, in the minds of some, was a remarkable resemblance, not in sentiment or substance merely, but in minute forms of expression, so that one might seem to have been copied from the other. Now on the natural though false assumption, that but one could be canonical, a view refuted by the obvious analogy of other scriptures,* it is easy to

* Compare Ps. 14 and 53; Ps. 18 and 2 Sam. 22; Isai. 36 38, and 2 Kings, 18.

---

§ 65. What remark applies to the four smaller catholic epistles? What may be said of Jude and 2 Peter in particular? Why is there really no ground for doubt or hesitation? What of 2 and 3 John? What is the result of these considerations?

imagine that the public judgment might be long embarrassed and divided, although finally convinced that each had held a place in the original canon. On the other hand, 2 and 3 John are both extremely short, being in fact the smallest distinct parts of the New Testament, and both in their immediate form and purpose very personal and private, and lastly both anonymous or half so, as the writer describes, but does not name himself. All these are reasons which in part account for the deliberation of the ancients in admitting these epistles to the canon, though entitled to a place there ab initio.

§ 66. Different as these cases are from one another, they are no less different from that of the Apocalypse (or book of Revelation) which is quite unique and sui generis. The main fact here is, that in tracing the books upward, after finding this one undisputed at the close of the fourth century, we come first to vague intimations, then to positive assertions, and at last to argumentative attempts at demonstrations, that it cannot be canonical; but passing on still further, we discover it completely

---

§ 66. How does the case of the Apocalypse differ from the others? How may this be stated in the reverse order? To what may the canonical history of this book be likened? How may its omission in the Peshito be accounted for? What modern analogy

reinstated, and the recognition of it more or less distinctly running back to the very age of the apostles. In other words, the book was first received by all, then suspected or condemned by some, and then again unanimously recognized as genuine. It simply suffered an eclipse, which like literal eclipses, was of brief duration, and has now been past for more than 1400 years. But how can we account for this eclipse—for this rejection of the book by certain Fathers, and for its omission in the old Peshito version? If this last fact be conceded, as it is not by all writers of distinction, a sufficient explanation is afforded by the circumstance, that versions of the Scripture were originally made, not for private circulation but for use in public worship, and that this book may have been omitted as unsuited to that purpose, though believed to be canonical, precisely as the Church of England now omits it almost wholly in her calendar of lessons, but expressly names it as a part of Holy Scripture in her articles of faith. A no less plausible and even satisfactory solution of the other fact in reference to this book, namely, its exclusion from the canon by some Fathers of the third and fourth cen-

---

throws light on this hypothesis? How may the rejection of this book by certain councils and fathers be explained? What shows this explanation to be the true one?

turies, is furnished by the well-known circumstance, that chiliastic doctrines of a very gross form then extensively prevailed, though constantly repudiated by the church at large, and so abhorred by some distinguished teachers that it tempted them to sweep away its alleged foundation by discrediting the part of Scripture which contained it. That this dangerous principle of exegesis was maintained and acted on by some, is certain; and that this great error was the cause of the eclipse before referred to, is apparent from the circumstance, that as soon as the obstruction offered by the chiliastic errors disappeared, or was reduced to harmless compass, the Apocalypse shone forth again with all its ancient but mysterious splendour.

§ 67. We have now seen that in reference to all these once disputed books, there is, to say the least, a possible solution of the doubts which once existed, perfectly consistent with their primitive and perfect canonicity, and, therefore, that we have no reasonable ground for refusing to accept the verdict of the church at the close of the fourth century, which put these seven books upon an absolute

---

§ 67. What is the general result of this examination? How does the evidence for the genuineness of those books compare with that for other ancient writings, such as the Apocrypha, the Apostolical Fathers, the Greek and Roman Classics?

equality, in this point, with the other twenty. Of the whole collection, thus restored to its original completeness and unity, it may now be observed, in conclusion, that the proof of its authenticity and genuineness far surpasses not only that of all apocryphal productions, which is saying nothing, nor that of any of the Apostolic Fathers, which is saying much, but that of any or of all the ancient writings in existence, with the single exception of the Hebrew Scriptures, which repose upon the same foundation, but without excepting the most valued and familiar of the Greek and Roman classics, whether Homer, Plato, Cicero, or Virgil, the identity of whose immortal writings no one ever dreams of questioning, though far less satisfactorily attested than the twenty-seven books of the New Testament.

§ 68. The reception of these twenty-seven books into the Canon is, ipso facto, the exclusion of all others which have ever claimed a place there, or have been considered as entitled to it. This definition or description comprehends two very different sorts of ancient writings, the *Apostolical Fathers* and the so-called *New Testament Apocrypha.* Some account of both will be given below, under

---

§ 68. What books are excluded by the settlement of the Canon? Where does the description of these books belong? What is the

the head of Hellenistic Literature.* All that is necessary here is to guard against a false assumption of some German writers, that all these books, canonical and apocryphal were promiscuously used at first, and on precisely the same footing, but that out of these the improving taste and judgment of the Christians finally selected those which constitute the present canon. This hypothesis, though plausible, and seemingly innocuous, would lead to very dangerous conclusions, making it impossible to separate the elements, and leaving us but one alternative—either that both are equally inspired or neither. The true state of the case is, that no books except those now contained in the canon, were entitled to a place there ab initio; that instead of the canonical books being chosen out of the whole mass of Christian writings, the apocryphal books arose from imitation of them. The great number of the latter goes to show the necessity of caution and discrimination in the ancient church, and to enhance the evidence in favour of the Canon as it now is, by contrasting the small num-

* See above, § 46, and below, §§ 129, 140.

erroneous modern view of the relation originally borne by these books to those now in the Canon? Why is this a dangerous hypothesis? What is the true state of the case as to the Canon and Apocrypha? How does this enhance the evidence in favour of the former?

ber of the books which it contains with the multitude which clamoured for admission, in the age succeeding that of the Apostles.

§ 69. Having now determined, in a general way, what book is entitled to the name of the New Testament, and what are the writings which compose it, we are ready for the next inquiry, as to the original language, or what is technically called *New Testament Philology.* That this is in its proper place between the Canon and the Text (§ 43) is plain, because until we have identified the book, we cannot ascertain the language; and until this is done, we cannot think of ascertaining the ipsissima verba, which of course have no existence even in the most exact translation. A familiar illustration may be borrowed from the case of one to whom a definite number of important papers have been solemnly entrusted for a certain purpose. The papers, it may be supposed, as well as the receptacle which holds them, are all sealed and labelled, and may thus be identified, before he opens them. But having ascertained that they are all in his possession, he proceeds to examine their contents, and, as the first step, to discover in what language they

§ 69. What is the second topic of General Introduction? Why is this its proper place in the arrangement of the topics? How may this be familiarly illustrated?

are written, and whether it is one with which he is acquainted; after which he may consider the particular expressions.

§ 70. If each of the twenty-seven books were written in a language of its own, or several in one and several in another, this whole topic would of course belong to Special Introduction. But as all the books, as far as we can trace them, are in one and the same language, what we have to say of it applies to the New Testament collectively, and therefore forms a necessary part of General Introduction. (§§ 18, 30, 33.) It is all reducible to four leading questions: 1. What was the original language of the New Testament? 2. Why was it different from that of the Old? 3. Why was Greek selected for this purpose? 4. What kind of Greek is used in the New Testament? The answers to these questions will constitute the topics of New Testament Philology, as we shall treat it—dwelling chiefly on the last, or the history and character of the Hellenistic dialect, in which the New Testament is written.

§ 71. The first question (what is the original

---

§ 70. Why does this topic necessarily belong to General Introduction? To what four questions may it be reduced? Which of these will require most attention?

language of the New Testament?) may seem superfluous, or answerable in a single syllable; but this has not been always an unanimous response. As examples of remarkable dissent from it may here be specified the notion of the Jesuit Harduin who, in his Commentary on the New Testament (1741), gravely insisted that all the books were written in Latin, except the Epistle to Philemon, which was written in Greek, then translated into Latin, and then retranslated into Greek. The motive of this singular paradox was no doubt to put honour on the Latin Vulgate, as declared to be "authentic" by the Council of Trent. A very different motive, the desire to escape from exegetical embarrassments, led Bolten, in his work on the Epistles (1800), to maintain that they were dictated by Paul in Aramaic, and written down in Greek by his amanuensis, whose errors of translation would account for most of the existing difficulties. Both these opinions are remembered only as curiosities of literary history. The questions still raised as to one or two books, more particularly Matthew's Gospel, belong properly to Special Introduction, and

---

§ 71. Why is the first question not superfluous? What was Harduin's notion? What was Bolten's? How are these opinions now regarded? How is the general fact affected by the doubts as to one or two books?

will there be fully treated. But even as to these books, it is not disputed that, so far as we can trace them, they have always worn a Greek dress, so that even if they were originally written in another language, which is not the case, as we shall see below, they can scarcely be regarded as exceptions to the general statement, that the whole New Testament is composed in Greek.

§ 72. The fact suggested by the second question (why was the New Testament written in a different language from the Old?) is not to be regarded as a matter of course, since all the antecedent probabilities were in favour of Hebrew as having been already used for the same purpose, and thereby specially adapted to it, as well as invested with a certain sanctity, over and above the prestige of its antiquity and claim to be regarded as the oldest of all extant tongues, if not the primitive language of mankind. To refer the adoption of another language in the Christian revelation to the sovereign will of God, is not explaining it, but simply a confession that it cannot be explained. The question is not whether God so willed it, which is absolutely

---

§ 72. What is the second question? Why is it not a matter of course? Why were the antecedent probabilities all in favour of Hebrew? Why is it not explained by a reference to the sovereign will of God?

certain, but whether he willed it for a purpose scrutable by us. If so, though under no necessity of knowing what that purpose is, we are at liberty to seek for it, and ascertain it, as an aid in solving other questions.

§ 73. The most satisfactory solution of this queston is, that each revelation was conveyed by the vehicle best suited to its purpose—the national and local revelation in the language of the chosen people—the œcumenical or universal revelation in the language of the civilized world. In the age of the Old Testament the Hebrew was moreover in itself the best adapted to the ends of a divine revelation; but at the close of the four centuries which intervened between the two, that language had not only never spread beyond the people who originally spoke it, but had ceased to be vernacular even among them; while the Aramaic dialect which superseded it had neither the prestige of great antiquity, nor special adaptation, nor the sanctity of long association, nor remarkable intrinsic qualities to recommend it.

§ 74. It may be objected to this explanation,

§ 73. What is the most satisfactory solution? What change had Hebrew undergone during the interval of four hundred years between the Old and New Testament? Why had the Aramaic no claim to succeed it?

that it makes an invidious distinction between the Old and New Testament, as if the latter only were designed for permanent and perpetual use. But this is a mistake very easily corrected by observing, that the difference in question has respect only to the primary form of the communication, not to its continued use; just as the form of Paul's epistles was determined by their being actually sent as letters to certain individuals and churches, though designed from the beginning to be permanently left on record for the use of all believers in succeeding ages. So, too, the Hebrew Scriptures, though originally meant for the instruction of a single race, and, therefore, written in a language never used as a vernacular by any other, were designed from the beginning to form part of a perpetual and universal revelation of the will of God to all mankind throughout all ages.

§ 75. To the third question (why was Greek selected as the language of the Christian revelation?) there is a twofold answer; one extrinsic, or derived from outward circumstances; one in-

---

§ 74. What objection is there to this explanation? How may it be answered? What analogy is furnished by the New Testament epistles?

§ 75. What is the twofold answer to the third question? What is the extrinsic reason?

trinsic, or arising from the qualities belonging to the language itself. The extrinsic reason is, because at the time of the Advent, it was the most widely spoken language in the world, and, therefore, the best fitted for this purpose, irrespective of its character and structure. The intrinsic reason is, that it was also the most perfect language in itself, and, therefore, doubly suited to become the vehicle of such a revelation, especially after it had been in use for ages as the language of the oldest version of the Hebrew Scriptures. (See below, § 95.)

§ 76. This preparation of a language for the Christian revelation must not be regarded as fortuitous, but providential, being part of an extensive preparation for the advent of the Saviour, going on for ages among Jews and Gentiles. This has sometimes been described by saying, that among the Jews, God prepared salvation for man (compare John 4, 22), and among the Gentiles, man for salvation; both negatively, by experimentally evincing the futility and worthlessness of heathenism, and exciting the desire of something better, and posi-

---

§ 76. How is this connected with the providential preparation for the Advent? How was it prepared among the Jews? How among the Gentiles? What was the negative preparation among the Gentiles? What was the positive preparation in general? What was it in particular?

tively, by providing vehicles and forms for the Christian revelation. The negative process here described, may be distinctly traced in the history of the most enlightened heathen nations, and especially in their condition at or just before the birth of Christ. The positive consisted partly in the general intellectual culture of the Greeks and others whom they influenced; partly in the gradual maturing of the Greek language to be used in the New Testament.

§ 77. The fourth question as to the original language (in what kind of Greek is the New Testament written?) presupposes the existence of more kinds than one, or in other words, implies that the language had experienced certain changes, or appeared in different forms, before it was made use of for this purpose. This makes it necessary to consider the origin and progress of the language, not in minute detail, but briefly, both for want of time, and because this part of the subject belongs rather to a previous stage of education, in which not only the language itself, but its history now generally occupies a prominent position. All that is necessary, therefore, is, a brief recapitulation of familiar

---

§ 77. What is the fourth question as to the original language? What does it imply or presuppose? What does this require to consider first? Why may and must it be considered briefly?

facts, or a rapid recollection of things previously known.

§ 78. In doing this it will be convenient to begin with the affinities of Greek and its position in the family of languages to which it properly belongs, as determined by Comparative Philology. The science designated by this phrase is one entirely of modern origin, having sprung up chiefly within half a century, but with a rapid growth, which has brought it to an almost instantaneous maturity. One of its marked results is an improvement in the scientific treatment of the several languages subjected to comparison, arising from the light which they mutually throw upon each other. Another is a gratifying confirmation of the statements found in Scripture as to the original oneness of the race, and of its language. Though all obscurities are not yet cleared up, this is the acknowledged tendency of all impartial and intelligent discussion and research, not only in Comparative Philology, but also in the kindred coeval science of Ethnology, or, as it is sometimes called, Ethnography. The way in which Comparative Philology contributes to this end is by showing the affinity of

---

§ 78. Where is it most convenient to begin this recapitulation? What is Comparative Philology? What effect has it had upon the study of particular languages? What is its tendency with respect

dialects apparently the most remote, and long regarded, even by the learned, as wholly and hopelessly heterogeneous. This again is brought about by exchanging the old fanciful and superficial etymologies founded on mere fortuitous resemblances of shape and sound, for a scientific and historical deduction, governed by fixed laws of permutation and analogy, and often leading to conclusions utterly unlike the premises or data, although rendered certain by an unbroken series of intermediate steps or changes. By this new and interesting process, forms of speech, the most dissimilar at present, may be traced back to a common origin, and thus the way prepared for an ultimate removal of the only serious obstruction to the identification of all known varieties of language, as diverging streams from one and the same fountain.

§ 79. Another fruit of the Comparative Philology of modern times, is the division of all cultivated language into two great families or stocks, excluding the Chinese and its derivatives, though spoken by a third part of the human race, as hav-

---

to the authority of Scripture? What other modern science coincides with it in this? How does Comparative Philology promote this end? How is this assimilation brought about? What may be expected from the further prosecution of this process?

§ 79. To how many families may cultivated languages be now

ing really no structure, in the ordinary sense of the expression, or at least as never yet successfully subjected to a thorough philological analysis. With this extensive and significant exception, all the cultivated languages of earth, meaning thereby such as have been written long enough to have a literature of their own, may be divided into two great classes. (I.) The *Semitic* (or *Shemitish*), chiefly spoken by the race of Shem, but also called the *Syro-Arabian*, *Hebraic*, and by several other names which need not be enumerated here, and (II.) *the Japhetic*, chiefly spoken by the race of Japhet, but more generally known by the comprehensive name of *Indo-European*, or the more specific one of *Indo-Germanic*, which at once suggests its vast extension from the Indian to the German Ocean, comprehending all the cultivated dialects of Europe, with several belonging to the south and west of Asia—the Sanscrit and its numerous derivatives—the Celtic, Teutonic, Scandinavian, and Slavonic dialects,—and intermediate between these the two classic languages of Greece and Rome. The Semitic family is far inferior, both in superficial measurement and

---

reduced? What is excepted from this classification, and why? What is meant by a cultivated language? What names have been given to the first of these great families? What to the second? What its extent? What languages does it include? What does the other family include?

number of affiliated languages, themost important being Hebrew, Chaldee, Syriac, Arabic, and Ethiopic.

§ 80. The most striking features of the Indo-European stock, by which it is distinguished from the other, are, first, the direction of the writing from the left hand to the right; then, the indiscriminate use of consonants and vowels, both as alphabetic characters and etymological elements; the less conspicuous position of the verb among the parts of speech, or rather of verbal roots, as the origin of other words; the absence of a definite and fixed form for these verbal roots, such as the triliteral [and dissyllabic]; the exclusion of gender from the verb, and its restriction to the noun and pronoun; the greater variety of temporal and modal forms; the disuse of prominal suffixes; and an almost unlimited fertility, boundless liberty, and freedom in all other kinds of composition. It is to the last two features—the variety of verbal and of compound forms—that the most developed and matured of the Indo-European tongues owe the flexibility and richness which distinguish them above all others.

---

§ 80. What are the most palpable and striking points of difference between these families of languages? Which of these peculiarities especially contribute to flexibility and richness?

§ 81. Among the errors which have been exploded by Comparative Philology is that which long prevailed as to the mutual relation of the two great languages of classical antiquity, it being now held by the highest philological authorities, not only that the Greek is not the mother of the Latin, but that it is probably not even an elder sister, as a living writer, of great eminence in this department, argues from the absence of the article in Latin and the smaller number of particles denoting the relations properly expressed by cases, both which peculiarities he looks upon as proofs of a later and more complete development of Greek, as we now have it.* But however this may be, the two are now regarded as collateral derivatives from a common stock, holding a central geographical position in this wide-spread family of languages, between its north-western and south-eastern limits, as well as in relation to their structure, being almost equidistant from the superabundant richness of the Sanscrit stem, and the comparative meagreness of some Teutonic branches.

* See Donaldson's New Cratylus, 2d edition (London, 1859).

---

§ 81. What ancient error has Comparative Philology exploded? What is now believed to be the true relation between Greek and Latin? What is Donaldson's argument for this conclusion? How much may be considered certain? What is the relative position of these languages, local and structural?

§ 82. The origin, both local and historical, of these important languages is hidden in obscurity; nor can it even be determined whether, or how far, they had a common basis in an older language ever actually spoken both in Italy and Greece. The two great elements of classic Greek, still commonly assumed, are scarcely known to us except by name, and that rather as an immemorial tradition than as the result of modern philological analysis. We only know, and only in this way, that the basis of the language was *Pelasgic*, and its later adventitious element *Hellenic*; but the origin of these names, with the local habitation of the mother tongue, and the date of the supposed amalgamation, are still subjects of conjecture and dispute, the settlement of which has thus far baffled the exertions both of philological and ethnographical research.

§ 83. It is a characteristic circumstance in Greek and Roman history, that the palmy period of the latter is the period of consolidation under one great central power, whether republican or im-

---

§ 82. What point is still involved in doubt, as to the origin of Greek and Latin? What is still assumed as to the elements of Greek? How (and how far) are they known to us? How far are they still uncertain?

§ 83. What is the characteristic difference of the Greek and

perial in form; whereas that of the former is the period of local separation into petty states, either hostile to each other, or at most united in a loose confederation. Whatever ground for this distinction may be found in the national character of these two races, the difference certainly exists, not only in their social and political condition, but even in their language, and particularly in the fact with which we are immediately concerned, that Greek, as far back as we now can trace it as a cultivated tongue, existed, not as one, but under several provincial forms, called Dialects.

§ 84. The origin and relative antiquity of these old dialects is so obscure, that even their number is a variable quantity, some writers recognizing more, some fewer, just as we might hesitate or differ in determining how many distinct dialects exist among ourselves, and still more in the British isles, where such diversities are far more numerous and marked. The highest philological authorities, however, seem agreed in retaining the old quadruple division, only discarding what the earlier writers called the Poetical Dialect, as something not dependent upon

---

Roman greatness? How far does it extend to the language? In what form do we first historically know the language?

§ 84. What doubt is there as to the old dialects? What one is repudiated by the modern writers? What is the twofold variation

local usage, but on literary fashion and prevailing taste. Omitting this, we may assume, in strict accordance with the latest philological research, as well as with an older usage, two original or primary variations in the language, and two subsequent or secondary, probably occasioned by extensive and remote migrations of the Greek or Hellenic race. The first two are the Doric and Ionic, one distinguished by its strength and harshness, and the other by its softer and more musical pronunciation, arising in a great degree, though not entirely, from a different combination and proportion of the consonants and vowels. After the settlement of Asia, in the proper sense, that is, the western provinces of what we now call Asia Minor, by Greek colonists, each of these ancient dialects received a colonial modification, the Asiatic counterpart of the Doric being the Æolic; while, on the other hand, the name Ionic, like its parent form Ionia, became fixed in Asia, and the Grecian branch of the same great dialect was called the Attic.

§ 85. The general difference between these Greek and Asiatic dialects was the same as that

---

commonly assumed? How are they related to each other? What were the two primary dialects? What was their characteristic difference? What were the two secondary dialects?

§ 85. How did they differ from the others? Were they any

between the tribes who used them, the Ionian and Æolian cultivation tending more to a voluptuous softness, the Doric and the Attic to a masculine severity. It is also important to observe, that these provincial dialects, although originally nothing more than local variations of the spoken language, became afterwards distinct types of expression and of composition, which were more or less promiscuously used, without regard to the writer's residence or nationality, as specially adapted to certain styles and subjects. Thus the Doric dialect was used all over Greece in choral, the Æolic in lyric, the Ionic in epic composition; while the Attic, though distinguished in every kind of literary labor, surpassed all the rest in its inimitable prose, which, in the writings of Thucydides, Plato, and the Orators, is still the highest model of combined strength and beauty, the most exquisite simplicity, and the purest taste. This marked superiority in that specific form of composition, which is more and more required and practised as civilization marches onward, was at once the cause and the effect of the extraordinary galaxy of genius by which Athens is immortalized. In other words, it was because her language was so perfect, that so

---

thing more than local variations in the spoken language? How were they used in different kinds of composition? How did the

many of her writers gained celebrity; and yet, it may be said with equal truth, it was because her writers were so highly gifted, that the Attic dialect attained the highest place by general consent, even while the states of Greece still remained aloof and independent of each other.

§ 86. The first great change from this condition, political and literary, was occasioned by the Macedonian ascendancy, in both its stages, the first under Philip of Macedon, the second under his still more illustrious son, Alexander the Great. Macedonia, lying on the northern boundary of Greece, and reckoned as belonging to it in the widest application of the name, was excluded from its stricter definition, and its people treated as barbarians by the national Hellenic pride, although the Greek descent of Philip and his royal predecessors was conceded, either as a subtle flattery, or in extorted admiration of his genius. By intrigue and influence, as much as by mere military strength, he gained an ascendancy in every Grecian state, and

---

Attic dialect surpass the rest? Of what was this both the cause and the effect? How early was this superiority acknowledged?

§ 86. What caused a change in the political and literary state of Greece? What was the first stage of the Macedonian ascendancy? How were the Macedonians and their rulers regarded by the Greeks? How did Philip of Macedon gain his ascendancy? What was its social and political effect? What was its effect upon

was finally acknowledged as the Protector of the whole, thus uniting the proud independent races, for the first time, in one nation, but purchasing this unity at the expense of all the local dignities in which they gloried. The analogous effect upon the language was to fuse its local variations into one *κοινὴ διαλέκτος*, of which the Attic was the basis, but to which the others all contributed their quota both of idioms and vocables. The conquests of Alexander carried some knowledge of this common dialect to the verge of India, and gave it permanent establishment wherever permanent Greek colonies were founded, and especially in those Greek kingdoms which were shared among the Macedonian generals, and preserved in a divided form the glories of that empire which existed undivided only seven years, and of that great conqueror who had personally no successor.

§ 87. Of these kingdoms, the most splendid on the whole was that of Egypt, where the Ptolemies succeeded one another, as the Pharaohs had of old. The importance of this new state was enhanced by

---

the language? What was the basis of the *κοινὴ διαλέκτος*? What was the effect of Alexander's conquests? Where was the Greek language introduced temporarily and permanently?

§ 87. Which was the most important of these Greek kingdoms in the East, and why? What was the position of Alexandria in the

that of the commercial mart established by the foresight and sagacity of Alexander, and distinguished, under his own name of Alexandria, for ages as a centre not only of commercial but of intellectual activity. As usual in all such cases, the activity of intercourse in trade, aroused and stimulated mental life; the confluence from all parts of the world increased it; Alexandria grew famous for its schools and libraries, among which was the greatest of the ancient world. Greek philosophy and learning here sought patronage or refuge from the decaying schools of Greece itself. It was in Alexandria that the race of Greek grammarians had its origin, whose soulless but invaluable labours first subjected the incomparable language to a microscopic criticism and minute analysis. These causes, in addition to their other manifold effects, could not fail to influence the language. It is still common to assume the existence both of a Macedonian and an Alexandrian dialect; the one produced by the Macedonian conquests, both in Greece and Asia, the other by the Macedonian reign in Egypt; though the traces of the former consist chiefly of a few detached words, said to be of Macedonian origin, and

---

ancient world? How was it distinguished in a literary way? What kind of learning had its origin and seat here? What effect had this upon the language? What was the Macedonian dialect? What

the latter first assumes a positive and independent character when afterwards developed as the Hellenistic dialect, by causes and in ways which we must now describe with some particularity.

§ 88. The next point to be considered is the providential means by which the Jews were brought in contact with the changes which have been described as flowing from the Macedonian conquests. The Greek kings of Egypt, in addition to their patronage of learning, took a lively interest in its inhabitants, contending with the Greek kings of Syria for the sovereignty of that diminutive but most important state, and when possessed of the ascendancy, not only favouring the Jews at home, but encouraging their emigration into Egypt, where extensive colonies were settled under the first Ptolemies, and a large proportion of the population of Alexandria was composed of Jews. This brought them into contact with the Greek civilization, and produced a mutual action and reaction between Judaism and Heathenism, not without perceptible effects upon both systems, or at least on some of

---

was the Alexandrian dialect? In what form was it afterwards developed? How must this form be considered?

§ 88. How were the Jews brought into contact with these changes? Who contended for the sovereignty of Palestine? What was the policy of the Ptolemies towards the Jews? What effect had this upon Judaism and Heathenism? What was the origin of

their adherents. This was the origin of the Sadducees or lax Jews, who inclined to assimilation with the cultivated Gentiles, in opposition to the Pharisees or rigid separatists not only in a social but a national sense. It also gave rise to that class of devout Gentiles whom we find in the New Testament and elsewhere, treating the religion of the Jews with serious respect, without in every case embracing it. Another fruit of these relations was a further modification of the language, which had now become the universal medium both of business and of literary intercourse. The idiom or dialect which thus arose is called the Hellenistic.

§ 89. According to the national tradition of the Greeks, once discredited as fabulous, but now again received as the best authority to which we can get access, the name usually given to the whole race (i. e. by themselves) was derived from that of *Hellen*, a son of Deucalion (the Noah of the classical mythology) who built a town in Thessaly to which he gave the name of *Hellas*, afterwards extended to the whole surrounding region, also called *Phthi-*

---

the Sadducees? What was that of the devout Gentiles? What effect had this upon the language?

§ 89. Who was Hellen? What was the primary application of the name Hellas? What were its secondary applications? How far was the name Hellen extended?

otis, or the country of the Myrmidons; then still further to the whole of Upper (or Continental) Greece, as distinguished from the Peloponnesus, or to Middle Greece, including parts of both; and finally applied to all countries settled by the Greeks, including Asia Minor and the part of Italy called Magna Græcia, in antithesis to which the mother country was sometimes spoken of as Old Greece (ἡ ἀρχαία ἑλλάς). By a similar extension, the name of the reputed founder was applied to his descendants, both in the singular and plural form (ἕλλην and ἕλληνες),* with the corresponding adjective (ἑλληνικὸς, comparative ἑλληνικώτερος) and adverb (ἑλληνικῶς), applied by Herodotus and Xenophon to the language, especially as purely spoken.

§ 90. Another derivative of Ἕλλην was the verb ἑλληνίζω, meaning to make Greek in any sense, as Thucydides applies the passive to a language (ἑλληνισθῆναι τὴν γλῶσσαι), then to be Greek, or to imitate the Greeks, in manners, institutions, sentiments, but specially in speech or language. The word was even used of native Greeks who paid particular attention to their diction, so that ἑλλη-

* Hesiod uses the form πανέλληνες, which also occurs in a suspected reading of the Iliad.

§ 90. What adjective and verb come from Ἕλλην? What verb?

νίζειν sometimes means to speak good Greek. But a much more common application of the term is to foreigners who spoke the language, whether well or ill. This imitation of the Greek or assimilation to them, both in the wider and the stricter sense, was ἑλληνισμός, while the person by whom it was practised was a ἑλληνιστής. This word also had its corresponding adjective and adverb (ἑλληνιστικὸς and ἑλληνιστί).* In its primary and wide sense, therefore, ἑλληνιστής denotes any foreigner who in any way followed the Greek fashion, but especially who used the language.

§ 91. As the Jews of the Diaspora in general, but more especially the Jews in Egypt, used the Greek language not only for colloquial but religious purposes as we shall see hereafter, they acquired a sort of twofold claim to the name Hellenist which in usage soon became appropriated to the Greek—as distinguished from the Hebrew, (or the Aramaic) speaking Jews. This specific application of

* See John 19, 20; Acts 21, 37, where it simply means *in Greek*. It is also used by Xenophon with ξυνιέναι.

How is it used? What nouns? What secondary adjective and adverb?

§ 91. Why was the name Hellenist applied particularly to the Jews? What was the opposite of Hellenist? How often does Hellenist occur in the New Testament? What does it evidently

the term occurs in the New Testament certainly once, probably twice, and possibly a third time. The undisputed case is Acts 6, 1, where a jealousy is said to have arisen in the infant church between the Hebrews and the Hellenists, to allay which seven deacons were appointed, all of whom have Greek names. Another almost equally clear instance is Acts 9, 29, where Saul is said after his conversion and return to Jerusalem, to have disputed with the Hellenists, or Greek-speaking Jews, to which class he belonged himself, and was therefore qualified to carry on the work, though he escaped the fate, of Stephen the first martyr. The only doubt in this case has respect to the true reading, which according to some copies is ἑλληνας, Greeks, i. e. natives or inhabitants of Greece, although the latest critics still retain the common reading (ἑλληνιστάς). A much greater doubt exists as to the third case, Acts 11, 20, where the external evidence preponderates in favour of ἑλληνιστάς and the internal in favour of ἕλληνας. In all these instances, the English version uses the form *Grecians*, to distinguish these Greek-speaking Jews from *Greeks* (ἕλληνας), which last form frequently occurs, but is

mean in Acts 6, 1? What does it mean in Acts 9, 29? What doubt as to the reading? What doubt as to 11, 20? How does the English version distinguish Hellenes and Hellenists? How is Hellenes sometimes rendered? How does the Peshito paraphrase

sometimes rendered *Gentiles* (e. g. John 7, 35. Rom. 2, 9. 10. 3, 9. 1 Cor. 10, 32. 12, 13). In the second of the places above quoted (Acts 9, 29), the Peshito (or old Syriac version) paraphrases ἑλλη-νιστάς as the Jews who knew Greek, and Chrysostom explains it as denoting τοὺς ἑλληνιστί φθεγγομένους). This is the sense in which I shall hereafter use the terms "Hellenist" and "Hellenistic."

§ 92. It follows from what has now been said, that the Hellenistic dialect or idiom is that form of the Greek language in which it was used by Jews, and as Alexandria was the point of contact between Greek and Jewish learning, this dialect is commonly regarded as a modification of the Alexandrian before described, arising from a greater or less mixture or infusion of a Hebrew element, whether derived from the vernacular of Palestine, or from the Hebrew Scriptures. The precise extent to which and way in which this Hebraic or Judaic modification of the Greek tongue took place is disputed, and will present itself again hereafter, for a more deliberate consideration.

Acts 9, 29? How does Chrysostom expound it? How will Hellenist and Hellenistic be applied hereafter?

§ 92. What is meant by the Hellenistic dialect or idiom? How did it differ from the other dialects? How was the Hebrew modification brought about?

§ 93. Had this dialect or idiom been merely oral, it would long since have shared the oblivion of their national or local variations in a spoken language. But what gives it interest and value now, is the fact that books were written in it, for a course of ages, and among them books of the highest importance. The aggregate of these books constitutes objectively, as the knowledge of them does subjectively, what is called "Hellenistic Literature," a branch of learning now distinctly recognized in our curriculum, and formally assigned to my department. It may be reduced to two great heads or classes, the Biblical and Non- (or rather Extra-) Biblical. A still more convenient distribution for our purpose, is the chronological division into periods or successive phases of this Hellenistic literature, as it still exists and may be traced in history.

§ 94. 1. The first of these forms is the Septuagint version of the Old Testament, anterior in date, by several centuries, to any other, and to which, as we shall see below, the Hellenistic dialect owes its distinctive character, if not its existence. 2. At-

---

§ 93. What gives permanent importance to this dialect? What is meant by "Hellenistic Literature"? To what two heads may it be reduced? How may it be chronologically divided?

§ 94. What is the first form or primary depository of Hellenistic

tached to the Septuagint version in most copies, whether manuscript or printed, are a number of writings, not translated from the Hebrew, but originally written in the Hellenistic dialect, and technically known as the Old Testament Apocrypha. 3. The third place in this chronological series of Hellenistic writings belongs to the New Testament itself. 4. Nearly contemporary, but a little later, and forming a distinct class by themselves, are the Jewish writers, Philo and Josephus. 5. Belonging to the same age, but of Christian origin, though uninspired, are the writings known in history as those of the Apostolic Fathers, on the verge of the first and second centuries. 6. Within the first half of the latter period fall such of the *New Testament Apocrypha* as were originally written in Greek, and which may be regarded as the latest samples of the ancient Hellenistic dialect, although it likewise forms the basis of the Ecclesiastical Greek, or that of the ancient Fathers after the Apostolical, and that of the mediæval or *Byzantine* idiom, and more remotely of the *Romaic* dialect now actually spoken and generally known as modern Greek. But these three latest forms of the Greek language lie beyond the limits of our present course, and will therefore

---

Literature? What is the second? What is the third? What is the fourth? What is the fifth? What is the sixth?

be excluded from the rapid view which I propose to give you of the other six.

§ 95. The oldest extant specimen or sample of the Hellenistic dialect and literature is the Septuagint version—by far the oldest biblical translation in existence—so old as to be in some sense an original. *Septuagint* is a slight abbreviation of the Latin *Septuaginta*, meaning *seventy*—corresponding to the Greek ἑβδομήκοντα—and often represented by the Roman numerals LXX. Of this ancient title there are two explanations, both of which agree in making seventy a round number for seventy-two, but one of which refers it to the Jewish Sanhedrim, either in Palestine or Egypt, by which the version is supposed to have been sanctioned; while the other and more common one explains it as the number of translators, handed down by an old tradition. This tradition exists in several different forms, the latter being generally more embellished than the older. From the close of the fourth century to the close of the seventeenth, there was a general acquiescence in the tale as told by Epiphranius, a learned and orthodox, but credulous

§ 95. What is the oldest specimen of the Hellenistic dialect and literature? What is the meaning of the name Septuagint, and what are its equivalents? How many explanations are there of this name? What is the one usually given? How is the tradition

and injudicious Father, who describes this version as the work of seventy-two men, who were shut up by pairs in six-and-thirty cells, and each translated all the books without the slightest variation. Two hundred years earlier Justin Martyr gives the same account, but varies it by mentioning as many cells as there were writers. Both these accounts imply that the translation was inspired, a fact explicitly affirmed by Philo, who says that being filled with God (or having God within), they prophesied (or spoke by inspiration).*

§ 96. The contemporary Jewish historian, Josephus, makes no mention of this circumstance, nor of the preternatural agreement of the versions, but gives a detailed account of the origin of the Septuagint, with accompanying documents. These are all derived however from another source, still extant, an epistle to Philocrates, purporting to be written by Aristeas, a courtier and friend of Ptolemy Philadelphus—and relating that Demetrius Phalereus, the librarian of that monarch, advised

* ἐνθουσιῶντες προεφήτευον. Philo de Vit. Mos.

---

given by Epiphanius? How is it given by Justin Martyr? What is Philo's statement?

§ 96. How does Josephus tell the story? Upon whose authority? Who was Aristeas? What is his account? Who advised the translation? What did Aristeas himself advise? What did the king

him to complete his collection of the laws of various nations, by adding those of Moses, or the Jews, and as these were written in an unknown character and language, counselled him to send for an authentic copy, and for competent translators from the Holy Land itself.* He accordingly sent two ambassadors, of whom Aristeas was one, and Andreas, the captain of his guard, the other. These went to Jerusalem, with letters and presents to the High Priest, who sent them back with a copy of the law written on parchment in letters of gold, and accompanied by six elders from each tribe, well acquainted with both languages. After being hospitably entertained for several days at court, they were conducted by Demetrius to an island, supposed to be that of Pharos, in the harbor of Alexandria, where they executed their task, not singly or in pairs, but jointly; the translation of each portion, when agreed upon, being written down in Greek by Demetrius himself. When their task

* Aristeas himself advised him to conciliate the Jews by ransoming the (100,000) Jewish slaves in Egypt, which he did, by paying 20 (Josephus says 120) drachms for each to the soldiers who owned them.

---

do? Who were the ambassadors? What did they take with them? What did they bring back? How were the seventy received and treated? Where did they perform their task? Who was their amanuensis?

was accomplished, they were sent home loaded with gifts and honours.

§ 97. There are some discrepancies in this account—e. g. as to the power by which the Jews had been enslaved, whether Persian or Macedonian—which, taken in connection with the obvious attempt to play the Greek, while all the style and sentiments are Jewish, have led the modern critics first to suspect and then to condemn this writing as a forgery—prompted by a wish to give ecclesiastical authority to a translation which might otherwise have seemed suspicious to the stricter Jews, as having been made in a foreign country, and under the auspices of a heathen king. This sceptical criticism has perhaps been pushed too far, as there is nothing intrinsically improbable in the story itself, which is certainly older than Josephus, whether written by Aristeas or not. That the version is of Egyptian origin, there is internal evidence; and although it was certainly in general use among the Jews there, this is not at variance with the fact of its having been prepared originally under the direc-

---

§ 97. What suspicious circumstances are there in this narrative? How is it regarded by the modern critics? What motive is imputed to the forgery? In what respect have the critics gone too far? What part of the story is entirely credible? What different purposes may this version have accomplished? What is the oldest

tion of the king, and for a political or literary, rather than a religious, purpose. The oldest undisputed testimony on the subject is that of Aristobulus, a Jewish Aristotelian in the reign of Ptolemy Philometor, some fragments of whose writings are preserved in those of Clemens Alexandrinus and Eusebius the historian, in which he says that the whole of the law was first translated into Greek under Ptolemy Philadelphus,* which may therefore be considered an established fact, and the germ of all the subsequent embellishments.

§ 98. The use of the ambiguous term *law* in these accounts, has raised the question whether it is to be taken in its wide sense as denoting the Old Testament, or in its strict sense as denoting the Pentateuch, or books of Moses. Josephus says expressly † that the latter only were translated by the seventy; ‡ but in the prologue to Ecclesiasti-

* Ἡ δε ὅλη ἑρμηνεία τῶν διὰ τοῦ νόμου πάντων.

† Ant. Prol. § 3.

‡ "Et Aristeas et Josephus et omnis schola Judæorum quinque tantum libros Moysis a lxx. translatos asserunt." Hieron. in Ezech. v.

---

undisputed testimony on the subject? Where is it preserved? What does it amount to? What may be considered certain, both from external and internal evidence?

§ 98. What question as to the extent of the translation? What is the Jewish tradition as recorded by Jerome? What is the testi-

cus,* the writer speaks of the law, the prophecies, and the other Scriptures, as existing in both languages. From this it is now commonly inferred, that the version was gradually made, having been begun under Ptolemy Philadelphus (or his father), and completed by the 38th year of Ptolemy Physcon, (B. C. 132).†

§ 99. That the version is the work of different hands, if not of different ages, is now very commonly agreed to be established by a marked diversity, not only of mere style and diction, but of ability and skill and knowledge, both of Greek and Hebrew. The most valuable portion is the Pentateuch, not only as the oldest, but because the Egyptian authors or translators were particularly

* Ὁ νόμος καὶ αἱπροφητεῖαι καὶ τἀλοιπὰ τῶν βιβλίων.

† 323 Ptolemy Soter (Lagi).
285 Ptolemy Philadelphus.
247 Ptolemy Euergetes.
222 Ptolemy Philopator.
205 Ptolemy Epiphanes.
181 Ptolemy Philometor.
170 Ptolemy Physcon.
117 Ptolemy (Soter) and Cleopatra.

---

mony of the son of Sirach? What inference is usually drawn from it?

§ 99. How does the plurality of authors appear? Which is the most valuable part, and why? Which part of the Pentateuch is

qualified for that part of the task. In the Pentateuch itself some distinguish as the best part the book of Leviticus, and in the rest the book of Proverbs, while the lowest place is unanimously given to the book of Daniel, which is so defective or absurd, that another version (that of Theoclotion) was early substituted for it in the copies of the Septuagint version.

§ 100. At a very early period, perhaps soon after it appeared, this version became current among the Hellenistic Jews, not only in Egypt, but in other countries, and, according to tradition, in the Holy Land itself. It was even introduced into the Synagogues, but probably not to the exclusion of the Hebrew text, which is still used by the Jews throughout the world in worship, though accompanied by vernacular translations for the benefit of those who are ignorant of Hebrew. A similar purpose was answered by the Septuagint in ancient times, when Greek was the language of the civilized world. It thus obtained extensive circulation, perhaps even among Gentiles, and was highly

---

best done? Which is the best of the other books? Which is the worst?

§ 100. How was the LXX. regarded by the Jews before the advent? How extensive was its use? Why did it not exclude the Hebrew text? What changed the feeling of the Jews respecting

valued by the Jews themselves, until the virulence of anti-Christian controversy led them to denounce it as an inexact translation, and fall back upon the Hebrew original, or on more accurate Greek versions, many of which sprang into existence in the first and second centuries of the Christian era. Three of these are known to us by name, those of Aquila, Symmachus, and Theodotian, and three others, which are nameless, but distinguished as the Fifth, Sixth, and Seventh, in the great work of Origen, the history of which, as well as of these versions, as such considered, belongs to Old Testament Literature. All that need be stated here is that all these versions have been lost, and now exist in fragments only, with the exception of the oldest, which has been preserved from the same fate by its ecclesiastical employment, first in the Synagogue and then in the Greek or Oriental Church, where it still maintains its ground, along with the original New Testament, and is the only one of these Greek versions which demands attention in the present course.

§ 101. The violent revulsion in the feelings of the Jews with respect to this time-honoured version

---

it? What did they use instead of it? How many other Greek versions are known to have existed? Why were they not preserved?

may be gathered from the foolish and extravagant expressions of the Talmud, e. g. that darkness overspread the earth when it was finished, and that the sin of making it was equal to the sin of making the golden calf. A like depreciation, though from other motives, and expressed in other forms, has resulted in our own day by reaction from the opposite extreme of idolatrous attachment which prevailed throughout the Christian world for ages, an extreme which still exists, though now comparatively rare.

§ 102. As a specimen of these extreme views may be cited the position occupied by Grinfield, one of the most learned Hellenistic scholars of the day, in his "Apology for the Septuagint" (London, 1850), namely, that the Septuagint version is inspired and precisely equal in canonical authority to the Hebrew text, or rather superior to it, on account of its affinity to the New Testament, arising from community of language, dialect, and diction, and from its being directly quoted in the New Testament itself. If such a theory could be established, it would revolutionize the whole work of criticism and interpretation by requiring them to

§ 101. What extravagant expressions are used in the Talmud? What extreme opinions have existed since?

§ 102. What is Grinfield's doctrine?

recognize a version and original alike and equally infallible, but in a multitude of cases quite irreconcilable.

§ 103. The arguments by which it is attempted to establish this extraordinary doctrine are in substance these: 1. The antecedent probability that with the change of dispensations from a local to an universal church, there would be a corresponding change in the language even of the older revelation, to adapt it to a new and more extensive use. 2. The fact that the New Testament was written in the very language of this ancient version, not only in Greek, but in the very kind of Greek, of which it furnishes the oldest sample.* 3. The derivation of the New Testament terminology from this source.† 4. The actual quotation from it, even when it differs from the Hebrew.‡ 5. The fact (alleged without proof) that our Saviour himself used this version from his childhood. 6. The fact (also asserted without proof) that German and American neology is owing to the neglect of Hellenistic learning, and exclusive study of the Hebrew Sciptures.

§ 104. In answer to these arguments it may be

* See below, § 109. † See below, § 110. ‡ See below, § 108.

§ 103. How is it supported?

stated first, that they either prove too little or too much, i. e. either that an uninspired version was sufficient for all necessary purposes, or else that the Hebrew text is wholly useless, being superseded by a version equally inspired, and therefore really a new revelation, as maintained in theory by several of the Fathers, and in practice by the Greek Church to the present day. In the next place, the original and version cannot be equally inspired, because if they were they would agree, and if it be alleged that either is corrupt, which is it, and why should it have been suffered to become so? All the arguments employed to prove the point go to show that the Hebrew text of the Old Testament is either sufficient or superfluous. It would be far easier to maintain, with some degree of plausibility, this last alternative, viz., that the Septuagint is not a version, but a new original, designed to supersede the old forever.

§ 105. Between these hurtful and extravagant extremes, there is a golden mean in which the learned, after many oscillations of opinion, have been gradually settling, a position equally removed from the error of the Christian Fathers, who re-

---

§ 104. How may these arguments be answered?
§ 105. What is the true mean between these opposite extremes?

garded the Septuagint version as a second revelation, by which the first had been legitimately superseded, and from that of the contemporary Jews, who, not content with rejecting its unauthorized pretensions to take precedence of the Hebrew text, repudiated and denounced it as an impious abomination. This conclusion naturally prompts the question, how shall it be reduced to practice?—or, what is the use to be legitimately made of the Septuagint version?

§ 106. The legitimate use of the Septuagint is twofold, in relation to the Old and New Testament. This is not a mere conventional distinction, but a radical and total difference, to show which it may be observed still more particularly, that the Old Testament use of this version is itself also twofold. In the first place, it is an important aid in determining the text of the Old Testament [though often misapplied in this way], by showing how these old translators read it. In the next place, it affords assistance in determining the sense, by showing how these old translators understood it. In other words, it is, when properly employed, a help both in Criticism and Interpretation.

---

§ 106. What is the twofold use of the Septuagint? What is its twofold Old Testament use?

§ 107. Now both these uses of the Septuagint version—namely, the Critical and Exegetical—are wholly inapplicable to the New Testament, which came into existence afterwards, and with whose text and meaning this old version can have no connection except indirectly, in a way wholly different from that in which it may be made to bear upon the Hebrew Scriptures. But, although not in the same sense or the same form, the Septuagint version is of no less value, possibly of greater, to the student of the New than of the Old Testament—and that in reference to three particulars which we shall specify.

§ 108. In the first place, the New Testament abounds in quotations from the Old, which are sometimes of the most important kind, such as prophecies fulfilled, or historical events explained, or general truths enforced by authoritative repetition. These quotations, which occupy a larger space than careless readers may imagine, are sometimes made directly from the Hebrew by original translation, but more frequently borrowed from the Septuagint version, as the one in common use, with

---

§ 107. Why are these uses inapplicable to the New Testament? How many uses has it with respect to the New Testament?

§ 108. What is its use with respect to the quotations?

or without modification. This brings that version into close connection with the Christian revelation, as the source of some of its most striking passages.

§ 109. But in addition to direct quotation, formal transfer of whole sentences or phrases from one part of Scripture to the other, there is a less prominent, but still more intimate, relation of the two, arising from community of language and identity of dialect. The basis of the Christian or New Testament idiom lies in the Septuagint version, and can never be elucidated fully without reference to it. In other words, it was the same peculiar form of Greek, which had its origin, or has its oldest extant exhibition, in this ancient version, that was afterwards adopted by the Holy Spirit, as the vehicle or costume of the new revelation.

§ 110. Lastly, although really included in the previous specification, it may be distinctly stated, on account of its important bearing both on interpretation and theology, that a large part of the religious terminology or phraseology which characterises the New Testament is really of older date, and may be traced to this old version of the Hebrew Scriptures,

---

§ 109. What is its philological relation to the New Testament?

§ 110. What is its technical use? How may this use be exemplified?

which had made many of these terms familiar to the Jews, long before they were incorporated into the language of the new or Christian revelation. As marked examples, serving to verify this general statement, may be mentioned the important terms, ἐκκλησίᾳ πρεσβύτερος.

§ 111. These important uses of the Septuagint version with respect to the New Testament, together with its value as the oldest form of Hellenistic composition, entitle it not only to a place in such a course as this, but to more assiduous attention as a part of ministerial training than it commonly receives. The best mode of supplying this deficiency, would be by connecting the study of the Septuagint version with the thorough philological analysis of the Hebrew Bible, so as to compare the two by one simultaneous (or immediately successive) process, an addition to our present theological curriculum devoutly to be wished.

§ 112. The grammatical study of the Septuagint version is facilitated now by cheap and accurate editions of the text (such as those of Tischendorf, Van Ess, and Valpy), and by the reference to Septuagint usage in the best Greek lexicons in common

§ 111. What is the best mode of studying the Septuagint?
§ 112. What are the best helps for such a study?

use, both general and special (such as Liddell & Scott's, Robinson's, &c.); while the means of more specific and minute investigation are afforded by the older works of Schleusner, Trommius, and others. [An effort to promote this study, on the plan above suggested, will be made, if practicable, in connection with the present course.]

§ 113. Next to the Septuagint or old Greek version of the Hebrew Scriptures, stands, in point of age and philological importance, as a source of illustration to the Greek of the New Testament, as well as a distinguishable form or phrase of Hellenistic Literature, a series or collection of ancient writings, known as the *Old Testament Apocrypha.** The argument against the canonicity of these books, belongs entirely to Old Testament Literature, or Introduction, and will be treated under that head, with as much particularity as circumstances may allow. In the meantime it may be assumed, as the conclusion of that argument, that all the books in question were uncanonical and uninspired.

§ 114. But though entirely without authority or

* See § 47.

---

§ 113. What is the second group of writings belonging to the Hellenistic Literature? What part of the subject must be here omitted as belonging elsewhere? What will be assumed ad interim?

use, as belonging to the Rule of Faith, these writings are entitled to attention from their great antiquity, their Jewish origin, and their Greek (or rather Hellenistic) dress. The salutary prejudice among most Protestants against them, as unjustly claiming or assigned a place in the inspired canon, should not be pushed so far as to prevent our making a legitimate and profitable use of them, as curious and ancient compositions, which contain some false doctrines, more false facts, and still more of false taste, but are, nevertheless, interesting; first, as sources or materials of history; then, as illustrative of Jewish manners and opinions in the interval between the Old and New Testaments; and 3dly, as throwing light upon the language of the latter; which last is the only reason for assigning them a place in any systematic course, however meagre and imperfect, of New Testament Philology.

§ 115. The fact just stated will require us to define with more precision the class of writings here referred to, some of which, if taken in the widest sense of the generic or collective term (Old Testa-

---

§ 114. Why are these books entitled to attention? What extreme or prejudice is to be avoided? What are the three uses to be made of these books? What especially connects them with our present subject?

§ 115. Which of the Old Testament Apocrypha have no such

ment Apocrypha), have no connection with our present subject, such as the 4th book of Esdras, and the 5th book of Maccabees (so called), which are not now known to exist in Greek at all, whatever may have been their original language. Of the much larger number which remain, some are certainly or probably mere Greek translations of Hebrew or Aramaic originals; but this does not impair their philological value as specimens of Jewish Greek or Hellenistic composition, any more than in the case of the Septuagint itself. For this reason, and because, with the exception of a single book (Ecclesiasticus), which is avowedly translated from the Hebrew, the evidence of this fact is exclusively internal and conjectural, it will be best to treat them all alike, merely observing, once for all, that besides the book just mentioned, those regarded by the latest critics as most probably translated from some other language, are the books of Tobit, Judith, and 1 Maccabees, together with the brief composition called the Prayer of Manasseh; whereas all the other books of Maccabees and Esdras (which exist in Greek), the book of Wisdom, the epistle of Jeremy, and the additions to Esther

---

connection? Into what classes may they be divided as to origin? Why is this distinction unimportant for our present purpose? How is the line drawn by the latest critics?

and Daniel, are now commonly regarded as original Greek compositions. The book of Baruch is referred by some to either class, the first half having indications of translation, which the latter half does not exhibit.

§ 116. As the term Apocrypha is somewhat vague, and the number of books comprehended under it not perfectly determinate, it may be useful for our present purpose to define it by restricting it to *those books which are found in the Septuagint version, but not in the original Hebrew.* How they gained admission to the Greek translation, where we find them intermingled with the canonical books, can only be conjectured. The most probable opinion is that the Greek or Hellenistic canon of the Old Testament, having no such protection as the Masora, or critical tradition of the Hebrew text, and the official or professional inspection of the Scribes, it was not always easy to determine whether books npon religious subjects, which were current among foreign or Greek-speaking Jews, were canonical or not; and as no authority existed out of Palestine to settle such disputes, some corruption became unavoidable.

. § 116. How may the Old Testament Apocrypha be conveniently defined? How did they gain admission to the Septuagint version?

§117. Although we are directly concerned only with the language of these books, and not with their intrinsic value, either literary or religious, it may not be amiss to observe, before proceeding further, that this value is as far as possible from being uniform or equal. On the contrary, the most remote extremes may here be said to meet, of eloquence and drivel, of the highest human wisdom and the silliest of nonsense. While the story of Susanna, and of Bel and the Dragon, are at best ingenious fables in the style of Scripture, and the larger books of Tobit and Judith mere domestic or historical romances, and the additions to Esther, with the books of Esdras, mere gratuitous additions to the corresponding parts of Scripture, the two books of Maccabees, and more especially the first, are almost the only sources of our knowledge as to the period of the Maccabees or princes. On the other hand, with many indications of the doctrinal corruption of the Jews, the moral books of the Apocryphas abound in noble sentiments and true philosophy immeasurably higher than the heathen standard, and often rising to a high degree of eloquence, not only in the Greek, but in the English version, made at the same time with that of the in-

§ 117. How do the books differ among themselves? Which are the best books, historic and moral?

spired Scriptures, and containing many words and phrases not to be found there, though all belonging to this well of English pure and undefiled. The two books, called Ecclesiasticus and Wisdom, are the most successful imitations of the style of Solomon that have ever been attempted, and perhaps approach as nearly to Ecclesiastes and the Book of Proverbs as any uninspired writings could at any rate, much nearer than would be attainable by even the most gifted modern writer. One of these aprocryphal, but ancient compositions, is retained, not only by the Church of Rome, but by the Church of England in her daily service, as the *Benedicite*, or Canticle, to be said or sung in place of the *Te Deum*, at the option of the minister.

OLD TESTAMENT APOCRYPHA.

§ 118. As to the use of these books in reference to the New Testament it is of course not intended to advise the expenditure of time and labor upon such aprocryphal productions in the case of ordinary ministers, but only to indicate a source from which the best writers now derive important illus-

---

§ 118. How are these books to be used by the student of the New Testament?

trations of the language and external form of the New Testament. At the same time there is a certain amount of general knowledge with respect to the Apocrypha which may be reckoned almost indispensable to every educated minister and critical student of the Scriptures. Of this I have given a mere outline which may be filled up by private reading as you find desirable hereafter.*

§ 119. The next group of Hellenistic writings includes those of Philo and Josephus, put together as belonging to no other class, and as living nearly at the same time, namely, Philo contemporary with our Saviour, and Josephus belonging to the next generation. Although both were Jews, yet eminent Greek writers, and, therefore, in the strictest sense Hellenists,† there could scarcely be two writers of the same class more unlike in their particular characteristics. They were not even residents or natives of the same country, and were wholly unlike in their literary tastes and predilections, the one connecting Jewish learning and religion with

* For a full description of the Apocryphal books, with the latest opinions in relation to them, see the 2d volume of Horne's Introduction (new edition.)

---

§ 119. What is the next group of Hellenistic writings? Why are Philo and Josephus classed together? How do they differ from each other?

the Greek philosophy, the other with Greek history. The one has been called the Jewish Plato, the other might be called the Jewish Xenophon.

§ 120. Of Philo's life we know but little beyond the fact that he was born and lived in Alexandria, where he enjoyed a high reputation both for eloquence and learning, and was sent, about the year 42, to represent the Jews of Alexandria at Rome, in opposition to a heathen deputation led by Apion, and commissioned to accuse the Jews before Caligula, who treated Philo and his cause with great severity, refusing even to let him speak, and even threatening his life. Later legends or traditions of the Church represent him as a convert to Christianity, and a friend of St. Peter whom he met at Rome, but as afterwards apostatizing. More authentic, no doubt, are the statements with repect to his high standing by Josephus and Eusebius.

§ 121. Philo's learning seems to have been wholly Greek, and chiefly philosophical. He is commonly supposed to have had no knowledge of the Hebrew language as he always quotes the Sep-

---

§ 120. What is known of Philo's history? What later legends with respect to him?

§ 121. What was the character of Philo's learning? What was

tuagint version, and sometimes betrays ignorance of the original. He is not considered an authority even with respect to Jewish usages and doctrines. The great aim of his life was to find the principles of Plato in the books of Moses, and thus to reconcile his philosophical convictions with his hereditary faith in the Old Testament. This could be accomplished, even in appearance, only by the most unnatural interpretations (*ἀλληγορίαι*) of the Cosmogony and Primeval History, as well as that of the Patriarchs, together with the Life and Laws of Moses. These are accordingly the chief topics of his extant works, consisting of detached pieces, or perhaps of one continued work divided by his copyists or editors. The abstruse and uninteresting character thus given to his writings has caused them to be little read or known in later times, the principal exception being those in which he gives historical information, as to the Therapeutæ and Essenes and as to his own embassy to Rome. On the other hand, his forced allegorical interpretations are supposed to have exerted an unfavourable influence, not only on the early heretics, but

---

his favourite object? How did he endeavour to accomplish it? What parts of Scripture did he thus allegorize? What is the form of his extant writings? Why are they little read? Which of them are most read?

also on the great Alexandrian school of Catholic Theology.

§ 122. From what has now been said it will be seen that Philo's writings are of more importance as a specimen and part of Hellenistic Literature, than from any practical assistance which they yield in the criticism or interpretation of the New Testament. That they are not wholly useless, even for this end, however, may be gathered from the long disputes respecting the Platonic Logos, as it appears in Philo's writings, and the influence exerted by it on the Christian terminology; as well as from occasional elucidations of particular expressions, where the classical and Septuagint usage fail us, and the only authority for certain senses is derived from Philo.*

§ 123. That we know far more of Josephus is owing partly to the popularity of his writings, partly to the gossiping and egotistical autobiography found among them. The main points of his

* See for example the verb κατοπτρίζω, as explained by Hodge on 2 Cor. 3, 18 (p. 76.)

---

§ 122. What is the chief value of Philo's writings? What do they illustrate in theology? How do they throw light on the Greek of the New Testament?

§ 123. Why do we know more of Josephus? What are the

history, as there recorded, are his high extraction (priestly on his father's side, and royal on his mother's); his great advantages of education in the Holy Land, and his unusual precocity in learning; his deliberate comparison of the three great sects or parties, and his final preference of the Pharisees; his embassy to Rome in behalf of certain priests whom Felix had sent there for trial; his success in this commission, and kind treatment by Poppæa, wife of Nero; his shipwreck in the Adriatic, with a company of six hundred; his advancement to important public posts at home, both civil and military; his settled opposition to the Zealots, and their consequent distrust of him; his masterly defence of Jotapata against the army of Vespasian for seven weeks; the loss of the place by treason, and his favourable treatment by Vespasian and Titus; his return with them to Rome, and then again to Palestine, and ocular witness of the Jewish war until the downfall and destruction of Jerusalem. The History of this War is his earliest production, and appeared about A. D. 75, in seven books, two of

salient points of his biography? What were his advantages of birth, education, and position? What points of contact with the history of Paul? What public stations did he fill? What was his relation to the Zealots? What was his chief military achievement? How was he treated by the Roman conquerors? How did he become a witness of the Jewish war? To which of his works did it

which contain a rapid sketch of Jewish history, from Antiochus Epiphanes to the appearance of Vespasian in the Holy Land; the other five, a most minute description of the war that followed, and of which Josephus was not only an eye-witness, but a *magna pars*.

§ 124. Eighteen years later (A. D. 93), he brought out his *'Αρχαιολογία Ἰουδαϊκή*, promised in his first work, and containing (in twenty books) an elaborate paraphrase of the Old Testament History, with occasional deviations and additions, perhaps founded on a national tradition, or derived from authentic sources, but in many cases, no doubt, merely conjectural or fanciful. After the close of the Old Testament, the history has more of an original and independent character, although it follows the books of Maccabees so far as they go. The period handled in the first books of the Jewish War is more particularly treated here, down to the

---

furnish a subject and occasion? When did this work appear? How is it divided? What is the subject of the two first books? What is the subject of the rest? What gives it great authority?

§ 124. What was his other great work? What is the meaning of the title? When did it appear? How is it divided? What is the first and larger part? What is its relation to the Old Testament history? What is probably the source of his variations and additions? How are they to be received? What is the value of the later part? What older history does it follow? What is common to both these great works of Josephus?

time of Gessius Florus, whose severities occasioned the great outbreak.

§ 125. A third work of Josephus, not to be confounded with the second, from the similarity of the title, is his Two Books against Apion, concerning the antiquity of the Jews as a nation, in which he vindicates the truth of sacred history, and the doctrines of the true religion, as he understood them, against heathen charges and objections. This work is valuable chiefly for the knowledge which it gives us of more ancient writings long since perished, such as the dynasties of Manetho.

§ 126. Besides the clear though incidental testimony which Josephus bears to the existence and the character of Christ and John the Baptist, he is almost our sole dependence for the last years of the Jewish state, and often useful as a commentator on the earlier history. His credit as a historian has fluctuated greatly. The contemporary Jews considered him a traitor to their cause, and accused him of falsifying history. This led their Christian opponents to the opposite extreme of overweening

§ 125. What third work of Josephus is still extant? What is its design? What is its chief value?

§ 126. What testimony does Josephus bear to Christ and his forerunner? What are the different opinions on the passage which

praise and confidence. Between these two extremes the opinion of the learned world has oscillated ever since. Some German writers do not hesitate to prefer his authority to that of the New Testament. Others argue from his flattery of Vespasian and Agrippa, that he cannot be relied upon. The present tendency, as in the case of Herodotus and other ancient writers, is to a more moderate and just appreciation of Josephus as a highly qualified and generally trustworthy witness, although not free from the common lot of weakness and corruption.

§ 127. The Jewish War was written, as we learn from himself, in the language of his country, and translated into Greek for the use of Gentile readers. As he makes no such statement with respect to the Antiquities, we may suppose that the interval of eighteen years, which he chiefly spent at Rome, enabled him to use Greek in the first instance. He affects Attic elegance in composition, but occasionally shows his Hellenistic origin. The writings of Josephus are among the most popular of ancient works. They and Plutarch's lives are constantly reprinted in cheap editions, and circulate even

---

relates to Christ? How may the historical uses of his writings be summed up? Why has his credit fluctuated? How is it at present?

§ 127. In what language did Josephus write? How far are his writings known to English readers?

among uneducated readers. Whiston's rude but faithful version is within the reach of all who read at all, both in the homeliest and in more attractive forms.

§ 128. The sixth group of Hellenistic writings (reckoning the New Testament itself as one) comprises what are called the Apostolic Fathers on the verge of the first and second centuries. The name of Apostolic Fathers has been given to those uninspired writers who were disciples, or at least contemporaries of the Apostles. There are seven usually reckoned, though the authenticity of several is still disputed. A full view of this subject belongs to the ancient period of Church History. Only so much of it will here be given as may be needed to complete our outline sketch of Hellenistic Literature.

§ 129. The first place in the catalogue is commonly assigned to Clement of Rome (or Clemens Romanus), represented by tradition as one of the earliest bishops of that church, and supposed to be

§ 128. What is the sixth group of Hellenistic writings? What is meant by Apostolical Fathers? How many are usually reckoned? Where does this history properly belong? How much of it will here be given?

§ 129. To whom is the first place commonly assigned? Where

the person named by Paul in his epistle to the Philippians (4, 3), as one of his fellow-labourers. An epistle of this Clement to the Church at Corinth was not only well known to the ancients, but actually read in public worship, but when this was discontinued, perhaps on the final settlement of the Canon, the epistle was lost sight of until re-discovered in the seventeenth century, as forming part of the contents of the famous Codex Alexandrinus, of which some account will be given in another place. It is an earnest exhortation to humility and concord, modelled upon Paul's epistles, but without much original or independent value. The same manuscript contains a portion of another composition under the name of Clement, commonly called his second epistle, but more correctly described as a homily or discourse, and of very doubtful genuineness, as it is not mentioned by the ancient writers, though it may be of the same age, and available in illustration of the later Hellenistic dialect. Other writings, once ascribed to Clement,

---

is he supposed to be named in the New Testament? What work of his is mentioned by the ancient writers? How was it then esteemed? What is its later history? What are its contents? What is its character? What other writing is ascribed to Clement? Why is its genuineness doubtful? How may it be used, whether genuine or not? What later writings have been falsely ascribed to the same person? Where does their history belong?

such as the Clementina, the Apostolical Canons, Apostolical Constitutions, and a few decretal briefs or letters, are undoubtedly of later date, and will be here left out of view entirely, as belonging to the ecclesiastical history and literature of succeeding centuries.

§ 130. Under the name of *Barnabas* there is extant an epistle which was certainly known to Clement of Alexandria, and which many still regard as the production of the Barnabas so often mentioned in the Acts of the Apostles and in Paul's epistles; while others infer from its allegorical interpretations of Scripture, and the disrespect with which it seems to treat the institutions of the old economy, that it is of a later date, and either a forgery (or pious fraud), or possibly the composition of some other Barnabas, erroneously confounded with the primitive missionary or apostle. Even Eusebius and Jerome regard it as apocryphal, i. e., not belonging to the Canon.

§ 131. Another name occurring in the New Testament, and also as the author of an extant writing, is that of *Hermas* (*Hermes*), named by

---

§ 130. What writing is ascribed to Barnabas? What are the opinions as to its author? What are the supposed indications of later date? How do Eusebius and Jerome regard it?

Paul in his epistle to the Romans (16, 14), and in the title of a book called the *Shepherd*, which we find referred to, as an ancient composition, by Origen, in the third century. It consists of three parts, the first of which contains four Visions, the second twelve Mandates, and the third ten Similitudes, the whole communicated by an angel in the form of a shepherd. This book, though fanciful and mystical, was highly esteemed in the ancient church, being often read in worship, and regarded as inspired by such men as Origen and Irenæus. The Muratori fragment before mentioned, represents it as the work of another Hermas, the brother of Pius, who was bishop of Rome about the middle of the second century. The intrinsic value of the work is small, and even its literary interest for us not great, as it now exists only in the form of a very ancient Latin version.

§ 132. The same thing is partially true of an undisputed writing of the same class, an epistle of

---

§ 131. Where is Hermas named in the New Testament? What work bears the same name? How far back may it be traced? How is it divided? What are the contents of the several books? What is the character of the whole? How was it regarded by the ancients? How by Origen and Irenæus? To whom is it ascribed in the Muratori fragment? What is its literary and religious value? Why is it comparatively unavailable for our immediate purpose?

Polycarp, bishop of Smyrna, a disciple of St. John, and an eminent martyr under Marcus Aurelius (A. D. 168). This epistle is addressed to the Philippians, and is valuable chiefly on account of its citations or references to the New Testament. Of the Greek original there are only fragments extant, but a complete Latin version.

§ 133. Ostensibly much earlier in date, but of far more doubtful authenticity, are the famous epistles of *Ignatius*, bishop of Smyrna, and martyr, under Trajan, which have been a subject of dispute for ages. The maximum number is fifteen, but a majority of these, five in Greek, and three in Latin, are now unanimously looked upon as spurious. The remaining seven exist in two forms (or recensions), a longer or a shorter, each of which is claimed to be the original by many learned writers. Within a few years a still shorter form in Syriac has been recently discovered, and is by some regarded as the original form, by others as a mere abridgment or mutilation of it, while a third class reject all three

---

§ 132. Who was Polycarp? When and how did he die? What extant writing bears his name? What is its chief value?

§ 133. Who was Ignatius? When and how did he die? What extant writings bear his name? What is the whole number of epistles? How many are now universally rejected? In what two Greek forms do the rest appear? What third form has been recently discovered? What different estimates are formed of it? What

recensions as alike supposititious. The epistles are remarkable for earnest opposition to certain forms of heresy, and zealous assertion of the Divinity of Christ, but chiefly for the zeal with which they urge the claims of the episcopate, and which has given them importance in connection with exciting questions of church-government. Whether written by Ignatius or not, their language is essentially the Greek of the New Testament, and therefore Hellenistic.

§ 134. Papias, bishop of Hierapolis (and martyr), like Polycarp, is said to have been a disciple of St. John, and a diligent collector of the sayings and doings of our Lord, as preserved by oral tradition. His book (*λογίων κυριακῶν ἐξήγησις*) exists only in fragments, preserved by Irenæus and Eusebius. The latter describes him as a man of little mind and a gross Chiliast, which error was extensively promoted by his writings.

§ 135. With these Apostolical Fathers, commonly so-called, is usually classed the anonymous writer of the Epistle to Diognetus, once ascribed to

---

are the characteristics of the seven Greek epistles? What has given them great interest in modern times? What is their philological character?

§ 134. Who was Papias? What book did he write? In what form has it been preserved? How does Eusebius describe him? What form of error did he help to propagate?

Justin Martyr because found among his works, but now regarded as of earlier date, and by one who describes himself as ἀποστόλων γενόμενος μαθητής. It is an eloquent defence of Christianity against the objections of an intelligent heathen friend, and is much more elegant in style than most Hellenistic writings.

§ 136. Not only as a specimen of Hellenistic literature, but as a connecting link between the Apostolical and later Christian writings, these works are entitled to attention on the part of ministers and others who are interested in the early church, though only few may be called to spend much time upon them. They have been translated into English more than once, the best known version being by an archbishop of Canterbury in the early part of the last century (Dr. Wake), who was disposed, however, to exaggerate their value. Among the editions of the original, there is a beautiful and cheap one in a single volume, edited by Hefele, a Roman Catholic professor of high standing.*

* Tübingen, 1847 (3d edition).

§ 135. What anonymous work belongs to the same class? To whom was it formerly ascribed, and why? How does the writer describe himself? What is the subject of the epistle? What is the character of its language?

§ 136. Why are these works entitled to attention? Where do they exist in English? What is the most convenient edition of the original?

§ 137. The last group of writings that can be regarded as belonging to the Hellenistic class, even in the widest sense of the expression, are the New Testament Apocrypha, a heterogeneous mass of forgeries or pseudepigrapha, which sprang up, with a rank growth, chiefly in the second century,* intended partly to maintain and propagate heretical opinions; partly to glorify the true religion by the unlawful means of pious frauds, but chiefly to fill up the supposed deficiencies and chasms in the canonical books of the New Testament. Of these writings none are strictly doctrinal in substance, and only one or two epistolary in form, such as the epistle to the Laodiceans, supposed to be referred to in Col. 4, 16, and a third epistle to the Corinthians, supposed to be referred to in 1 Cor. 5, 9; to say nothing of the pretended correspondence between Paul and Seneca, or that between our Lord himself and Abgarus, king of Edessa. Some of these writings are pretended prophecies, ascribed to heathen

* Epiphanius mentions thousands of Gnostic Apocrypha, and Irenæus found, among the Valentinians alone, *inerrabilis multitudo apocryphorum et perperam scripturarum.*

---

§ 137. What is the last group of Hellenistic writings? What do Irenæus and Epiphanius say as to their number? When do they most abound? What were their various designs? Are any of them doctrinal? Which are epistolary in form? Which are prophetic? What apocryphal apocalypses are there?

seers (as the Sibylline books, in Homeric hexameters), or to real characters in sacred history, such as the Book of Enoch, the Testament of the Twelve Patriarchs, the Ascension of Isaiah, all which contain express predictions of the Saviour and the Christian Church.*

§ 138. But most of these Apocrypha are histories, intended to supply the omissions of the Gospels or the Acts. Some, no longer in existence, but referred to by the ancient writers, such as the Gospel of the Hebrews, that of the Egyptians, that of Peter, that of Marcion, seem to have been mere corruptions of the canonical four gospels, made for the use of heretical sects. Others, still extant, and more properly denoted by the name Apocrypha, do not purport to be complete histories of Christ, but only supplements relating chiefly to his childhood and his passion. Of the former class, the oldest and the least extravagant is that called the Protevangelium of James the Less, designed to glo-

* There are also spurious apocalypses under the names of Peter, Paul, Stephen, Thomas, and even John himself, all of which appear to have been more or less absurd imitations of the genuine Apocalypse.

---

§ 138. To what class do the most belong? What were the Gospels of the Hebrews, the Egyptians, Peter, Marcion, &c.? What parts of the Gospel History do the extant Apocrypha pretend to

rify the Virgin Mary, not only as the Mother of our Lord, but by relating her whole history. Another of the same general character is the Gospel of the Nativity of Mary, purporting to be written by Matthew and translated by Jerome. A third is the history of Joachim and Anna, the nativity of Mary, and the infancy of Christ, chiefly occupied with miracles wrought by him in the flight to Egypt. A fourth is the history of Joseph the Carpenter, which dwells chiefly on the circumstances of his death, of which we have no account in the New Testament. Far more absurd than these is the Gospel of the Saviour's infancy, containing a multitude of silly and unmeaning miracles. Still worse is the Gospel of Thomas, which pretends to give the life of Christ, from his twelfth to his sixteenth year. The character of these books is evinced by their attempting to supply those omissions which especially illustrate the veracity and wisdom of the true evangelists, and in a way as destitute of taste and common sense as of religious spirit and historical authority.

---

give? What is the Protevangelium of James? What is the Gospel of the Nativity of Mary? The history of Joachim and Anna? The history of Joseph the Carpenter? What is the Gospel of the Saviour's Infancy? The Gospel of Thomas? What is the characteristic difference between these and the canonical gospels?

§ 139. The other class of apocryphal gospels professes to complete the closing part of our Lord's history, by furnishing additional details as to his passion. The Gospel of Nicodemus undertakes to give a formal record of the proceedings before Pilate; an account of two of the resuscitated saints referred to by Matthew, 27, 52, and described as sons of Simeon; and a description of our Lord's descent into hell. The Acts of Pilate is a name borne by three distinct works, only one of which is extant. The first was very ancient, being mentioned by Justin Martyr and Tertullian, and contained a report made by Pilate to Tiberius; a communication of the latter to the Senate, proposing to place Christ among the gods; and a letter of Tiberius to his mother. The second Acts of Pilate were of heathen origin, containing blasphemous perversions of the history as given in the Gospels. The third, still extant, like the first, though far posterior in date, purports to be a statement made by Pilate to Tiberius of the miracles, death, and resurrection of the Saviour. To these may be added an account of Pilate's punishment, and an epistle of Lentulus to the Roman Senate, containing a description of

§ 139. What is the other class of apocryphal gospels? What is the Gospel of Nicodemus? How many books have been entitled Acts of Pilate? What did the first contain? What was the

Christ's personal appearance.* The epistle of Lentulus also originated in the middle ages, and several of the others are but little older, while a few of those first mentioned approach very nearly to the time of the apostles, and a large proportion are most probably not later than the second century, which may be regarded as the most prolific period of this supposititious literature.

§ 140. It is worthy of remark that in this whole collection or farrago, there is not one book, however small, which approaches in literary or religious value to the better books of the Old Testament Apocrypha. Indeed they may all be described as intrinsically worthless, and indebted for whatever adventitious value they possess to their indirect bearing on the genuine New Testament. Their use in this respect is threefold. 1. In the

* There were many apocryphal lives of the Apostles current in the third and fourth centuries, chiefly of Gnostic origin and tendency. The fullest collection (that of Tischendorf) contains thirteen, of which seven have been recently discovered. The latest in date is the Historia Certaminis Apostolorum, which, though containing older materials, is probably as late as the ninth century.

---

second? What is the one now extant? What other writings of the same class? What Apocryphal Acts are there?

§ 140. How do these books compare with the Old Testament Apocrypha? What is their intrinsic worth? What is their adven-

first place, they illustrate, by a glaring contrast, the perfection of the Scriptures, in comparison with writers of the same race and religion, and in some cases almost of the same age. Even the Apostolical Fathers answer the same purpose of exhibiting the difference between inspired and uninspired men of the same general character and class; but the contrast is vastly more instructive as presented in these obvious imitations and professed improvements on the sacred record.

§ 141. In the next place, they illustrate the discretion, care, and even critical skill, with which the ancient church preserved the sacred Canon and asserted its exclusive claims against so many, and such impudent, competitors. Not that the present Canon is, as some allege, a gradual selection made, as taste and judgment were improved, from a promiscuous mass originally equal in their claims and estimation—which would leave us no alternative but that of making all inspired or none—but because these wretched imitations, all posterior in date to the Canonical Scriptures, by their intrinsic

titious value? How do they enhance that of the Canonical Scriptures? Why more so than the Apostolic Fathers?

§ 141. What bearing have they on the question of the Canon? What is the false view of their original relation to it? To what dangerous conclusion does it lead? What is their true relation to it? How do they corroborate the external testimony in its favour?

meanness or absurdity, confirm the judgment of the ancients which excludes them from the Canon, and corroborate the external evidence in favour of the twenty-seven books which now compose it.

§ 142. In the last place, these Apocrypha, intrinsically worthless as they are, possess a certain literary interest, as samples of the language and the dialect employed in the New Testament. But this, which is their only claim to notice here, has reference of course only to such books as now exist in Greek, whether as originals or versions. Some, which were written in that language, are now extant only in translations, e. g. the Ascension of Isaiah, in Ethiopic; the Epistle to the Laodiceans, in Latin; the third to the Corinthians, in Armenian; the Historia Certaminis Apostolorum, in a Latin version of a Greek version of a Hebrew original; the History of Joseph, in an Arabic translation from the Coptic; the Nativity of Mary, in a Latin translation from the Greek; the Gospel of the Infancy of Christ, in an Arabic translation from the Syriac, &c. Some—e. g. the History of Joachim and Anna, the Acta Pilati, as now extant, &c.—seem to be Latin originals, while only a few,

---

§ 142. What is their philological use? To which of them is this restricted? How differ as to language? Which of them do not

but those the oldest, and in other respects the most important—such as the Protevangelium of James, the Gospel of Thomas, and of Nicodemus, the Anabaticon of Paul, the Testament of the Twelve Patriarchs, and the Sibylline Oracles—appear to have existed always in a Greek form. It is only with these, therefore, that we are concerned, as affording illustration to the Greek of the New Testament, and constituting the last class of writings which can be considered as belonging, even in the widest sense of the expression, to the field of Hellenistic Literature. [Besides more general and costly collections of the New Testament Apocrypha, Tischendorf has published critical editions of the spurious Acts and Gospels, each in an elegant octavo volume].

§ 143. Having now surveyed the Hellenistic Literature in its outlines and its principal divisions, we return to our main theme, the Greek of the New Testament, and to the question, what kind of Greek it is? Before considering it for ourselves,

---

exist in Greek at all? Which are Latin originals? Which are Greek originals? Where are the New Testament Apocrypha collected?

§ 143. What is the question now before us? What historical inquiry still remains? How far back must it be carried? What was the state of learning in the middle ages?

it will be well to glance at the history of opinion with respect to it, involving that of a most curious and protracted controversy, the results of which are still perceptible in this important field of sacred learning. To make this narrative intelligible, it will be necessary to begin as far back as the Reformation—or rather in the period of darkness which preceded it, and during which ancient learning, as well biblical as classical, was banished from the Church by the universal prevalence of scholastic dialectics and metaphysical theology.

§ 144. The great religious revolution, which we call the Reformation of the sixteenth century, was preceded and promoted by an intellectual or literary revolution, known in history as the Revival of Letters, i. e. an awakened interest in ancient, and especially in Greek and Latin, learning. A mighty impulse was imparted to this movement by the conquest of Constantinople by the Turks, and the downfall of the Eastern Empire (A. D. 1453), which scattered educated Greeks all over Western Europe, and especially through Italy, who thus became the teachers of the western nations, and by exciting an enthusiastic zeal for the Greek classics, produced

---

§ 144. What is meant by the Revival of Letters? What great political event hastened it? How?

indirectly an analogous effect in favour of Latin and even Hebrew studies.

§ 145. The Revival of Letters, although providentially conducive to the greater Reformation which ensued, was not itself a religious movement. Some of its leaders, especially in Italy, were open infidels, and some affected to desire the restoration of the classical mythology. Even Popes and Cardinals could talk and write about the gods as familiarly as any ancient heathen. And some, who did not go so far, still sought the revival of letters for its own sake, whence the whole class took the name of *humanists*, or devotees of *Literæ Humaniores*, as distinguished from the barbarous scholastics, or illiterate priests and monks of the same period, some of whom are said to have denounced the Hebrew Bible and Greek Testament as recent and heretical inventions.

§ 146. Some of the Humanists, especially in Germany and Holland, from previous habit or ecclesiastical position, gave particular attention to the Biblical part of ancient learning; a few, such as Caprio or Reuchlin, to the Hebrew Bible, and a

---

§ 145. Was the Revival of Letters a religious movement? What was the religious spirit of some of its leaders? Who were the Humanists?

greater number to the Greek Testament, editing the text, translating, annotating, with the great advantage of familiar acquaintance with the Greek and Latin classics. The most eminent of this class was Erasmus, the most elegant of modern Latin writers, a devoted admirer of the Greek classics, to whom the world is indebted for excellent translations and editions of the Fathers, for the earliest series of Greek Testaments, on which the common text is founded, and for a paraphrase of the New Testament still unequalled in that kind of literature.

§ 147. But Erasmus, while contributing in this way to the Reformation, was a Humanist at heart, devoted more to learning than religion, and measuring even the Scriptures by a classical and heathen standard. It is not surprising, therefore, that with all his devotion to New Testament criticism and interpretation, he could speak of a "sermo apostolorum, non salum impolitus et inconditus, verum etiam imperfectus et perturbatis, aliquoties plane solœcissans," and that later writers, far less compe-

---

§ 146. Who were the Biblical Humanists? Who was the most eminent among them? How did he contribute to the reform?

§ 147. What were his real motives? What was his highest standard? How does he describe the style of the New Testament? How was this idea carried out by others?

tent to judge, and less entitled to be heard, spoke in still more exaggerated terms of the solecisms and barbarisms of the sacred writers, arising from their ignorance of classic Greek, and from their Jewish education.

§ 148. Far more moderate and just was the judgment of two other eminent Greek scholars of the sixteenth century, Theodore Beza and Henry Stephens, also connected with the history of the text of the New Testament. The former, in writing on the gift of tongues, admits the Hebraisms of the sacred writers, but regards them as beauties (gemmas) and as more expressive of the truth than any other forms of speech could be. The latter, in the preface to his edition of 1576, gives the same decision, and exclaims against those "qui in his scripturis inculta omnia et horrida esse putant." But, notwithstanding these authorities, the supercilious judgment of Erasmus still continued to be echoed by a series of inferior writers.

§ 149. This continued through the sixteenth century, and the first quarter of the seventeenth, but then a violent reaction took place, marked by

---

§ 148. What was the testimony of Theodore Beza and Henry Stephens? How was it opposed by others?

§ 149. How long did this opposition last? What reaction fol-

the appearance of Sebastian Pfochen's Diatribe de linguæ Graecæ Novum Testamentum puritate (Amsterdam, 1629), followed by other writers upon both sides, two of the ablest being Heinsius for, and Gataker against, the Greek of the New Testament; while Olearius and Leusden held the middle ground, that although it had many Hebrew idioms, and a general Hebrew modification, it was still Greek. The controversy lasted a whole century in the Reformed Church, and then began afresh in the Lutheran, where it continued many years.

§ 150. The extreme grounds taken by the Hebraists and Purists, as these parties called themselves, were equally untenable; the one maintaining that the Greek of the New Testament was no Greek at all, but a barbarous Jewish jargon; while the other held that it was pure and elegant according to the highest classical standard. Both proceeded also on fallacious principles; the Hebraists assuming that the presence of strange idioms and of a local tinge could destroy the identity of the

---

lowed? What may be regarded as the opening of the strife? Who followed on both sides? What middle ground was taken, and by whom? How long did the controversy last, and where?

§ 150. What were the parties called? What were their extreme grounds? What was the false assumption of the Hebraists? What was that of the Purists? Why was bad Greek "not derogatory to

language; the Purists that it was derogatory to the Scriptures to admit that they contained bad Greek. This was only true upon the supposition that by "bad" was meant a language not adapted to answer its great purpose of expressing thought and conveying truth, but not if it merely meant the violation of some conventional factitious standard; just as a house would be too *bad* for a church, if men could neither see nor hear nor obtain shelter in it, but not if it were only bad in the æsthetic sense of not being Gothic, with pointed arches and painted windows. These extremes conduced to the ultimate triumph of the middle ground already mentioned, and which was finally expressed in Ernesti's dictum, that the Greek of the New Testament is composed of a classical and Hebrew element, and that they are only to be pitied who maintain that it is all good Greek [that is, according to the Attic standard].

§ 151. One incidental good resulting from this long and apparently pedantic quarrel, was the vast accumulation of real or pretended Hebraisms on the one side, and of classical parallels upon the other, which could only be collected in the course of

---

the Scriptures"? In what case would it be so? What is the real case? How may this be illustrated? Which opinion ultimately triumphed? What was Ernesti's dictum?

many years and by a multitude of hands, and which have since afforded the materials of many valuable works, such as Lambert Bos on the Greek Ellipsis; various illustrations from the usage of particular Greek writers by Raphelius, Kypke, Schoetgen, Valckenaer, Krebs and others; and the later lexicons and grammars, some of which will be particularly mentioned in another place. (See below, § 162).

§ 152. Since the days of Ernesti the old school of Purists has been quite extinct, and that of extreme Hebraists nominally also; but there has not been wanting a strong tendency, especially in writers of a lower rank, to multiply such idioms unduly, and to seek them where some other explanation is sufficient and more natural. The great reformer of this last abuse is George Benedict Winer, the chief glory of whose life is the success with which he has defined and held possession of the true mean between all extremes, rejecting equally unfounded claims to classical correctness and gratuitous assumptions of exotic idioms, where the

---

§ 151. What incidental good arose from this controversy? What important works have thus been brought into existence?

§ 152. What has been the state of the question since Ernesti? What abuse has still been practised? Who reformed it?

form of speech is really pure Greek, or common to all cultivated languages.

§ 153. It is important to observe that the merit of Winer did not lie in the discovery or demonstration of any new principle, but simply in applying, with consummate skill, the one already fixed as the result of the investigations and discussions of the two preceding centuries, reducing the number of alleged Hebrew idioms on one hand, and on the other reaffirming some which the Purists had denied. This process, from its very nature, can be only an approximate one, as men of equal learning and capacity may still differ as to the existence of a foreign idiom in a given case, and no man's judgment can be absolutely binding upon others as to all such cases, though undoubtedly correct in most, especially when uttered by a writer of such philological precision, logical intellect, severe taste, and superior tact, as all acknowledge to have met in Winer.

§ 154. Another fact of some importance in defining his position, is, that while he fully recognized the language of the New Testament as genuine or

---

§ 153. What was and was not Winer's real merit? Why could not his work be absolutely finished? What were his qualifications for it?

real Greek, the identity of which could not be vitiated by its pervading Jewish tinge or Hebrew idioms, especially when these had been reduced at least to probable dimensions; he still denied to it the name of a Greek dialect, and gave it the generic one of Idiom (Sprachidiom), by which he seems to mean the aggregate of insulated and detached departures from the standard of a strictly correct usage, having no organic unity or common character, arising from the action of like causes, as in the case of local or provincial dialects, like those of ancient Greece. And yet the germ of this last theory is found in Winer's own great work, but only as it were in passing, and without a due effect upon his practice. The full development of this idea in its bearings upon exegesis, was reserved for younger and less practised hands.

§ 155. To H. J. Thiersch is commonly assigned the praise of having first broached, or more probably matured, the now prevailing notion of the Greek of the New Testament, as a co-ordinate and independent dialect, determined in its origin and character by causes quite analogous to those which

§ 154. What did Winer still deny as to the Greek of the New Testament? What is the difference between idiom and dialect? Where is the germ of the modern doctrine to be found?

§ 155. Who first developed it? What is the new theory?

brought into existence the old dialects of Greece itself, and equally productive in both cases of a substantive, organic oneness, as remote as possible from simple aggregation of peculiar idioms, whether few or many.

§ 156. This, though it may not seem so at first sight, is a decided step in advance of the old doctrine, even as exhibited by Winer, and of great importance in its bearing on the critical and learned study of the Christian Scriptures. It is one thing to regard their confessed peculiarities even as innocent or unavoidable departures from the standard of correct Greek usage, and quite another thing both in itself and in its influence upon the student, to regard the same peculiarities as part and parcel of a definite local and provincial dialect, as truly living and as truly Greek as the Attic or Ionic. The most admirable thoughts expressed in broken or exotic English, may command our intellectual respect and moral reverence, but cannot possibly excite our literary or æsthetic admiration, and although this is not essential to the highest ends of language, it materially lessens its enjoyment by the

---

§ 156. Why is this an advance even upon Winer's doctrine? State the difference between them? How may this be illustrated from our own language? How may the illustrations be applied?

reader, in proportion to his native taste or cultivation. So in the case before us, the most firm believer in the inspiration of these writings, may be pardoned for perusing them with less zest, of a literary kind at least, when he believes them to be written in genuine but bad Greek, even in the lower sense of this expression, than when he is permitted to regard them as invaluable samples of a dialect as noble, in its way, as Attic or Ionic.

§ 157. I say as noble in its way, because it would of course be preposterous to claim for it the qualities described as Attic purity, Ionic suavity, or Doric strength; for these are to be measured by a standard of their own, which is esentially conventional and artificial, because resting on a variable taste and usage. But in reference to the highest end of language, to convey thought and reveal truth, this despised patois, as some have deemed it, may be just as perfect as the Greek of Plato; while in reference to the truths revealed, they are immeasurably higher; and this grandeur of the thoughts conveyed cannot fail to dignify and sublimate the vehicle itself. No language, even the

---

§ 157. In what sense must the Hellenistic be inferior to the Attic and other ancient dialects? In what sense may it be superior? How may this be illustrated by analogy?

most meagre and inelegant, can be successfully employed for the expression of the highest truths, without being in itself ennobled. If an ordinary missionary, who translates into the jargon of some African or Indian tribe, the sublimest doctrines of the true faith, thereby changes its whole character, how could such an one as Paul, in the power of his logic and the fervour of his eloquence, controlled and prompted by his inspiration, fail to bring even Attic Greek still nearer to perfection, at least as the expression of those glorious truths, which neither Plato nor Demosthenes, if suddenly apprised of them, could possibly have uttered.

§ 158. We may safely rest then in the paradoxical but just conclusion of some recent German writers, both philologists and church-historians, that the Greek of the New Testament may claim not only a co-ordinate position with the old Greek dialects, as an organic form of the same language, but a place still higher, when considered as the dress, the channel, or the vehicle of saving truth. At the same time we may question or repudiate the undue refinements of the same school in attempting to discriminate the shifting preponderance of the

---

§ 158. What is the conclusion of the latest German writers? With what caution must it be received?

classical and Hellenistic elements, not only in the different books, but in the same books when the tone or subject changes.*

§ 159. It is this noble dialect, of Greek extraction, but of Christian birth, the history of which we have been thus far tracing, and the main peculiarities of which we must now philologically analyze. These peculiarities fall into two great classes, the Lexicographical, relating to the sense of words, and the Grammatical, relating to their formal changes and syntactical construction. In investigating both it is the part of wisdom both to save time and facilitate the process by resorting to those writers who present with most authority and clearness the results of the great controversy which has been described, and the gigantic labours which grew out of it. From the earlier and more minute attention paid at first to lexicography, these helps are more abundant with respect to this department than to that of grammar.

* This caveat is necessary even with respect to the admirable chapter on the subject in Schaff's History of the Apostolic Church (German ed. § 134, English ed. § 153).

---

§ 159. How are we now to investigate this dialect? How may its peculiarities be classified? How may we best conduct the investigation? In which department are the helps more numerous, and why?

§ 160. Leaving wholly out of view the many works of older date, which have now been superseded and almost forgotten, I may mention as the first direct attempt to gather up the fruits of the great controversy, *Schleusner's Lexicon in N. T.*; originally published in 1792, soon after the solution of the long vexed question, and in a fourth edition, 1819, during which period, of nearly thirty years, it was the standard and authoritative work, though more remarkable for crude and undigested learning than for scientific method or exact philology. Superior in both, as well as in the richness of its classical citations, was the *Clavis N. T. Philologica* of *Wahl*, the first edition of which synchronizes with the last of Schleusner (1819), while a third appeared as late as 1843. But long before this there arose a new lexicographer, *Bretschneider*, whose *Lexicon Manuale in N. T.* (first edition, 1824; third edition, 1840), performed the same work as to Hellenistic writers which had been performed by Wahl as to the classics. The *Clavis N. T. Philologica* of *Wilke* (1841), is simply an improvement upon both these in philological com-

---

§ 160. What may be entirely omitted in enumerating the helps? What was the first lexicon which presented the results of the great controversy? What was its influence? What were its defects? What was the peculiar merit of Wahl? What of Bretschneider?

pleteness, but without any very novel features of its own. All these were neologists or rationalists, more or less decided. Soon after the appearance of Wahl's first edition, it was translated into English by Dr. Edward Robinson, now of New York, then of Andover (1825), who, ten years later, published a lexicon under his own name (1835). What he had done for Wahl, Dr. S. T. Bloomfield did for him, i. e. he edited Robinson's lexicon in London (1837), and a few years after brought out one of his own (1840), the latest edition of which (that I have seen) appeared in 1845; that of Robinson in 1850. None of these books should be allowed to supersede the general Greek lexicon in study; first, because the latter gives a wider view of classical usage; and secondly, because the former exercise too much authority in exposition, although less suspected than avowed interpreters.

§ 161. Into the scale against these many lexicons, I throw a single grammar, the *Grammatik des Neutestamentichen Sprachidioms* of *Winer* (first edition, 1822; sixth edition, 1855), which, for a full third of a century, a whole generation of

---

What is the character of Wilkes' Clavis? What was the religious position of the men? What was the origin of Robinson's lexicon? What was that of Bloomfield's?

§ 161. What has been the one standard Greek for the last

human life, has been unanimously recognized in Germany, and more slowly in other countries, as the standard and authoritative exposition of the theory which has been described already as the final product of the Hebraist and Purist controversy. Besides an English version of the first edition by Professors Stuart and Robinson, and a New Testament grammar of the former, based on Winer's, but intended to answer the purpose of a general Greek grammar, the original work was translated in this country about twenty years ago, but was found to be so hastily and incorrectly executed, that its use has long been discontinued. A new translation by Edward Masson, M. A., "formerly professor in the University of Athens," has appeared this year in England, and simultaneously in Philadelphia. This translation is far superior to the other, and as nearly perfect as is necessary for our purpose.

§ 162. Out of Winer's grammar, some years after its appearance, Professor Stuart framed an elementary Greek grammar, intended to embrace the valuable substance of the former, but without original or independent value. In 1842 appeared

third of a century? When was it first translated? What became of this translation? Who has recently translated it? Where has it been republished?

in England a Treatise on New Testament Grammar, by Thomas Sheldon Green, an accomplished classical scholar and teacher, not claiming to be a complete system, but full of profound grammatical philosophy and nice discrimination, illustrated by a wide and copious reading of the classics, and although wholly independent of Winer (of whose existence it betrays no knowledge), constantly tending to the same conclusions, and sometimes going further in the same direction.

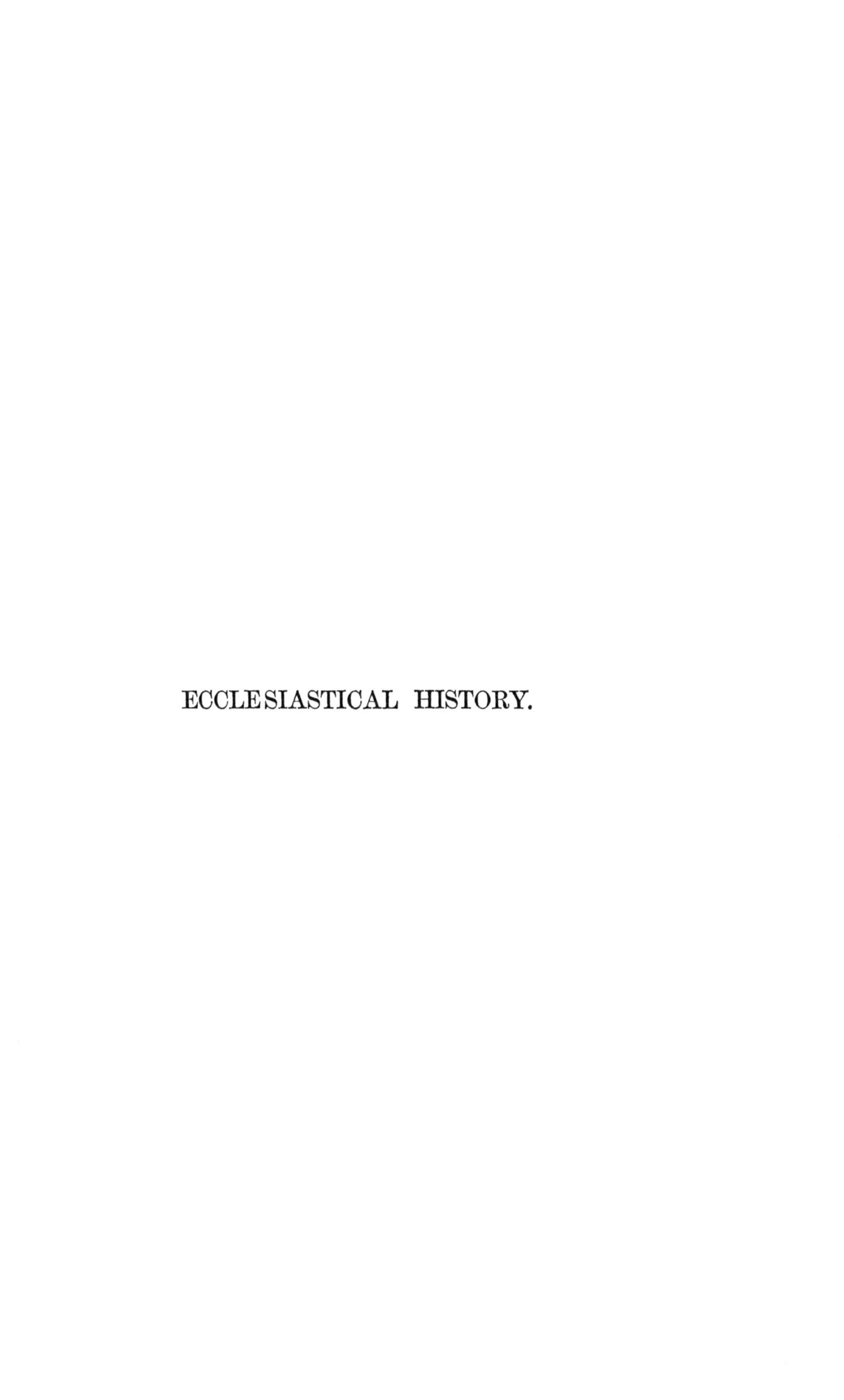

ECCLESIASTICAL HISTORY.

ECCLESIASTICAL HISTORY.

§ 1. The most important preliminaries to this study may be conveniently reduced to six heads or topics—1. Definitions. 2. Relations. 3. Uses. 4. Sources. 5. History. 6. Method.

§ 2. The first of these includes the answer to two questions—(*a*) What is ecclesiastical history?—(*b*) How far does it extend?

§ 3. In all such cases it is best to begin with the etymology of terms, when this can be determined without recondite research or fanciful conjecture.

§ 4. The English word *history* is derived, through the Latin *historia*, from the Greek ἱστορία, which, according to its etymology and primary usage, denotes *information*, knowledge gained by inquiry, with particular reference to matters of fact, and by a further limitation, to events or actual occurrences.

§ 5. This last is the invariable usage of our own word, perhaps with the single exception of the technical phrase "Natural History," in which the term retains its original and wider meaning.

§ 6. Some modern writers make a distinction between *Objective* and *Subjective History*, the first denoting the events themselves, the second their recital or exhibition, either *viva voce* or in writing.

§ 7. When we say that prophecy is verified in history, we use the word in its objective sense; but when we say that the prophecies of Daniel are elucidated by the history of Greece, it is subjective.

§ 8. It is only with subjective history that we are concerned as a science, or a subject of instruction, which may be defined the science of events, or the methodical and rational investigation of what has actually taken place; the methodical or systematic form distinguishing history, properly so called from chronicles or annals, which are mere collections of historical material.

§ 9. History, as thus defined, is necessarily unbounded, and can never be exhausted, since something may be added still to the most copious historical account, even of a day or hour.

§ 10. It follows that all history must be eclectic, in the sense of presupposing or involving a selection from the great mass of accessible materials.

§ 11. The vast field of history may be reduced, without detracting from its value, by the twofold process of (*a*) Elimination and (*b*) Division.

§ 12. Elimination, as here used, is the exclusion of some element, belonging to the subject in its widest definition, but not essential to its practical utility or purpose.

§ 13. We may thus eliminate from history, as a subject of investigation, all that does not relate to the human subject, such as natural history and angelic history, as well as all that relates merely to the individual, and constitutes Biography, so far as this can be distinguished from History, of which it is, in fact, a species.

§ 14. Division differs from Elimination in excluding no entire element of history, but merely one or more of its parts, by an arbitrary or conventional arrangement.

§ 15. Such division may be merely mechanical,

as in the case of Ancient and Modern History, which differ not at all in kind, but only in chronology; or rational, as in the case of National History; or that of particular professions, sciences, or doctrines.

§ 16. Among the innumerable possible divisions of General or Universal History, one of the most obvious and important is the old distinction between Civil and Religious History, the first relating to men's temporal interests and mutual relations, the second to their spiritual interests and relations to their God, which cannot be entirely divorced, but may predominate in different degrees, so as to give character and name to these two kinds of history.

§ 17. Under the genus of Religious History, the most extensive and important species is the History of the Church, which is indeed almost the same thing, since all the topics of Religious History may be included in Church History, except perhaps the history of personal religion and a few particulars of still less moment.

§ 18. The meaning of the phrase "Church History," or rather its extent of application, will depend upon that of the term "Church," which although absolutely used to mean the Christian Church, as such, admits of a much wider application.

§ 19. The word *church* has been derived by some from a Celtic root (*cyrch* or *cylch*) meaning *centre* and then rallying-point or rendezvous; but much more probably by most writers from a Greek phrase (*οἰκία* or *ἐκκλησία κυριακή*) meaning the Lord's House or Congregation.

§ 20. We are concerned with it, however, only as a modern version of a Greek word (*ἐκκλησία*) derived from a verb (*ἐκκαλέω*) meaning to evoke or call out, but suggesting also the idea of convoking or calling together as an organized body.

§ 21. The Greek noun is applied in the classics to the political or legislative bodies of the Grecian states, particularly Athens; in the Septuagint version of the Old Testament, to the congregation of Israel, considered as the chosen people; and in the New Testament, to the same body as reorganized on a Christian basis at the day of Pentecost.

§ 22. The widest application of the phrase "Church History" depends upon the question, how long there has been a body in existence corresponding to the essential definition of *ἐκκλησία*, i. e. one called out from the mass of men, and called together in a separate society, by divine authority, and for a religious purpose.

§ 23. It is evident from Scripture that such a society existed long before the day of Pentecost, before the Advent of our Lord, before the Babylonish Captivity, the reign of David, the Conquest of Canaan, the Mosaic Legislation, the calling of Abraham, the Universal Deluge.

§ 24. Its existence may be traced back to the Protevangelium, or first promise of a Saviour (Gen. 3, 15), with the accompanying prophecy of mutual hostility for ages between two great parties, "the seed of the serpent," represented by Satan, and "the seed of the woman," represented by Christ.

§ 25. The fulfilment of this prophecy gives colour or complexion to all history, in which the opposition or antithesis of Church and World can be distinctly traced from age to age, beginning with the contrast between Cain and Abel, followed by that between the posterity of Cain and Seth, until confounded by the impious amalgamation of the "sons of God" and "daughters of men," which led to the general corruption of mankind and their destruction by a deluge; then reappearing in the family of Noah and the line of Shem, made still more marked by the calling of Abraham, to be the father of a separate race, and permanently fixed by the Mosaic legislation, ceremonially distinguishing the chosen people, even externally, from every other, till the Advent of Messiah and the change of dispensations.

§ 26. Since then a church or chosen people has existed in all ages, the idea of church history must be equally extensive, reaching from the Fall of Man, or his ensuing restoration, to the present moment, and this last is a variable fluctuating point, it is continually growing in extent, as every day adds something to the field and the materials of history.

§ 27. The extent of the subject being still unmanageably great, it may be conveniently divided, not by a mechanical and arbitrary process, but on principles arising from its very nature.

§ 28. The primary division is into two great parts, which may be designated *Biblical* and *Ecclesiastical History*, the latter comprehending all that is not recorded in the Word of God.

§ 29. The difference between these two parts is not merely circumstantial, but essential, being that between inspired and uninspired history; a ready-made authoritative record, and one to be constructed from diversified materials by human skill and labour; the one requiring mere interpretation, while the other calls for a dissimilar and far more complicated process. The application of the same mode of treatment to materials so unlike, has always been the cause or the effect of sceptical misgivings, if not of avowed unbelief in the divine authority of Scripture.

§ 30. As an additional facility in study and investigation, Biblical History may be subdivided into that of the Old and that of the New Testament, although the difference is here a circumstantial one, implying no diversity of inspiration or authority, but only one of date, language, and specific form, requiring some diversity of method for the illustration and interpretation of these two great subdivisions of the Sacred History.

§ 31. The three divisions of Church History thus arising (Old Testament, New Testament, and Ecclesiastical), are exceedingly unequal in their chronological dimensions, the first comprising about forty centuries, the third eighteen, the second less than one, but claiming full equality of time and attention, on the ground of its absolute importance, springing from the dignity of its subject, the Life of Christ and the Acts of his Apostles, and on that of its relative importance, as the winding up of the Old Testament History, and the foundation of Ecclesiastical History, without which both would be incomprehensible and worthless.

§ 32. According to these definitions and distinctions, *Ecclesiastical History* is the third great division of *Church History* in the widest sense, beginning at the close of the New Testament Canon, or rather of the history which it contains, and reaching to the present time, or stretching indefinitely into the future.

§ 33. The relation of Ecclesiastical History, as thus defined, to Biblical or Sacred History, is not coincident with that between the history of the New and of the Old Dispensation, since a part of both these is contained in the New Testament, the Gospels belonging to the one, and the Acts of the Apostles to the other; so that the limit of the two economics or dispensations does not fall between the Old and New Testament, but between the two historical divisions of the New.

§ 34. This brings us to the second introductory question (see above, § 1), namely, what relations does Ecclesiastical History sustain to other sciences or fields of knowledge?

§ 35. Besides its relation to Biblical History, which has just been defined, it has points of contact with a multitude of subjects, some of which are so near akin to it, and practically so inseparable from it, that they may be classed together as its cognate or auxiliary sciences. The nearest and most necessary of these helps, to which the name just mentioned has been commonly applied, are three in number: 1, Geography; 2, Chronology; and 3, Archæology.

§ 36. *Historical Geography* relates to the localities of history, and ascertains the places where events occurred; and is therefore a subordinate auxiliary science, since the interest of the places depends upon that of the events, and not *vice versa.*

§ 37. The same thing is true of Chronology, the science of dates, as these derive their value from the events, of which they fix the time, and not the events from them.

§ 38. The principal uses of *Historical Chronology*, so called to distinguish it from that which is merely arithmetical or astronomical, are to solve apparent contradictions, and to determine the mutual relation of events, especially as causes and effects, or antecedents and consequents.

§ 39. That the absolute chronology, i. e. the precise day or even year, of an event, however interesting it may be and worthy of attention when it can be ascertained, is not essential to historical truth or to its beneficial uses, may be seen from the familiar fact, that men not unfrequently forget the exact dates of their own biography, without losing their distinct impression of its principal events in their mutual relations and their true succession; or, to borrow Bossuet's illustration, from the slight effect of the acknowledged error in the Christian era on the history of the last eighteen hundred years.

§ 40. *Archæology* (from ἀρχαῖος, ancient), the science of antiquity (hence called by the Latin name *Antiquitates*), in its widest sense embraces ancient history, as in the Jewish Archæology cf Josephus; but in its technical restricted sense, relates to usages or permanent conditions, as distinguished from events, which always involve change, so that nothing immutable can have a history, and the best times to live in are the worst to write about.

§ 41. This distinction, being artificial and conventional, cannot be rigidly insisted on, since archæology and history are partially inclusive of each other, and are always interchanging their materials, events becoming usages by repetition, and permanent conditions being liable to change, and thus continually passing from the field of archæology to that of history.

§ 42. But even if they could be kept apart, their total separation would be undesirable, since they are necessary to illustrate and complete each other; and accordingly the best historians are disposed to reunite them, by admitting much into their histories which formally belongs to archæology, as in Macaulay's famous chapter on the change of manners and the mode of life in England, which is one of the most brilliant and instructive portions of his history.

§ 43. Ecclesiastical Antiquities or Archæology is limited by arbitrary modern usage to the government and worship of the Church in the first six centuries; but recent writers give it more extension, among whom may be mentioned a learned and laborious American scholar (Dr. Lyman Coleman).

§ 44. The moderns, and especially the Germans, are accustomed to distinguish many other auxiliary studies, such as that of *Statistics*, exhibiting the actual condition of the world, or any of its parts, as to population, industry, wealth, trade, &c., *at a given time*, in which it differs both from History and Archæology; *Diplomatics*, or the art of decyphering and verifying documents; *Historical Philology*, distinguishing the dialects of different localities and periods; and many others, which it is not necessary to enumerate, as such distinctions, if pursued too far, tend to defeat their own design by comprehending every thing, especially in this case, where the principal subject, that of History, has really so many points of contact with the other provinces of human knowledge. (*Vide supra*, § 35.)

§ 45. In answer to the third preliminary question —What are the uses of Church History? For what reason or what purpose, is it to be studied?— the utility of history in general may be argued from the space which it occupies in Scripture, and from the position assigned to it in the literature of the wisest and most cultivated nations, as well as in every scheme of liberal study, which together may be represented as the testimony or the judgment of the civilized world throughout a course of ages.

§ 46. The maxim that "history is philosophy teaching by examples" has sometimes been abused, by making it the basis of specific prophecies or prognostications, which are usually falsified by the event; but this abuse does not destroy the lawful use of general experience, as a source of correct judgments in relation to the future; just as long practice may be an invaluable guide to the physician, though it does not enable him to predict with certainty the issue even of a single case.

§ 47. Of history in general, and of ecclesiastical history in particular, it may be said, that they illustrate, in an eminent degree, the laws of the divine administration; evince the truth of prophecy by showing its fulfilment; and in due subordination to the study of God's word and of our own hearts, furnish the best school of human nature, although commonly postponed to that of frivolous society and superficial worldly wisdom.

§ 48. In addition to these benefits of all authentic history, that of the church contributes to the demonstration of the truth of Christianity, by contrasting it with every form of error, by recording its triumphs over enemies and obstacles which seemed invincible, and by showing its invariable moral influence where it prevails; all this in spite of human errors and corruptions, not only in the world, but in the church itself.

§ 49. Among the salutary moral influences which have been ascribed to the judicious study of this subject, may be named the elevation and enlargement of the views beyond the petty bounds of personal, sectarian, or local interests; the consequent discouragement of bigotry, and moderation of mere controversial zeal, without impairing men's attachment to the truth itself; and lastly, the suppression of crude innovations, both in theory and practice, by showing that the same, if not in form in substance, have been canvassed and exploded centuries ago. But independently of all utilitarian considerations, authentic history, as well ecclesiastical as general, demands attention on account of its intrinsic value, as a portion of that truth, which is the natural and necessary aliment of mind, and which would be entitled to regard on this ground, if it had no other practical effect whatever.

§ 50. The fourth preliminary question (*vide supra*, § 1), is, From what sources, or of what materials, is Ecclesiastical History to be constructed?

§ 51. It may be answered, in the general, first, that according to the very definition above given (§ 29), all the authorities are uninspired; and, secondly, that they are incalculably numerous and endlessly diversified.

§ 52. In order to a more particular and positive solution of this question, the materials and sources of Ecclesiastical History have been divided into two great classes: 1st, Monumental; and, 2d, Documentary.

§ 53. To the first class belong all historical materials or authorities not contained in books, including monuments, not only in the narrow sense of tombs or sepulchres, but in the wide sense of relics or memorials of antiquity, particularly buildings, statues, paintings, medals, coins, inscriptions.

§ 54. Authorities of this class, when extant and accessible, have this advantage, that they are originals; whereas, the oldest books now extant are mere copies of copies.

§ 55. The utility of monumental sources or authorities may be exemplified by the arch of Titus, still standing at Rome, with the original carvings, representing the triumph of the conqueror of Jerusalem, from which are derived our common drawings of the sacred vessels and utensils of the temple, as carried in procession upon that occasion; and also in a less degree by the inscriptions upon ancient Christian tombstones, which are built into the wall of a gallery of the Vatican museum, and by which some light is cast on early customs and conditions of society.

§ 56. In Ecclesiastical History, however, Monumental sources and authorities are neither so abundant nor so valuable as the Documentary, or those contained in books or other writings, whether manuscript or printed.

§ 57. These may again be subdivided into, 1st, Private or Personal; and, 2d, Public or Official.

§ 58. By Public Documents, in this connection, are meant all official acts of public bodies or authorities, having direct or indirect ecclesiastical influence or jurisdiction.

§ 59. The first place among these is due to the acts of councils, ecumenical or national, who claimed to represent the Church, and in her name decided questions both of discipline and doctrine.

§ 60. Some idea of the vast extent of these materials may be gathered from the fact that besides a collection of these Acts of Councils in four folio volumes, and another in twelve, there is one in eighteen, one (the best, that of Mansi) in thirty-one, and one in thirty-seven folios; not to mention smaller works, containing only national or local councils, such as Wilkin's Concilia Magnæ Britanniæ et Hiberniæ (4 vols. fol.).

§ 61. Another class of these material, inferior in authority, but of great historical value, are the Acts of the Popes, or of the Papal See—the Regesta—the Corpus Juris Canonici—the Briefs—the Bulls—and the Decretals.

§ 62. To give some idea, as before, of the extent of these materials, it may be stated that, although the Regesta, prior to the close of the twelfth century, are lost, those belonging to the next four centuries are said to be preserved in the Vatican library at Rome, in two thousand folio manuscript volumes, which have never been accessible to Protestants, except in a solitary case, and then to a very limited extent.

§ 63. A third class of public documentary materials are those contained in the archives or records of civil governments in Europe, some of which go back to the old Roman times, and all of which contain ecclesiastical matter, in consequence of the intimate connection between church and state since Constantine.

§ 64. Still more direct in their bearing on Church History are the collections of Symbolical Books, including Creeds, Confessions, Catechisms, and other books of elementary instruction in the doctrines of religion, which of course afford important aid in tracing theological mutations.

§ 65. Similar light is thrown upon the history of worship, and indirectly upon that of practical religion, by the ancient liturgies, which, far from being uniform and homogeneous, are both numerous and various in a high degree.

§ 66. Of less intrinsic value, but of great historical importance in relation to particular periods, are the rules and statutes of religious bodies, such as the Regulæ, or Constitutions of Monastic orders, which exerted a great influence upon society, and often give the key to circumstances otherwise inexplicable.

§ 67. This is not proposed as an exhaustive

catalogue of public documentary materials, but rather as a sample of the most abundant sources, which may serve to convey an imperfect but definite idea of the multitude of such materials, which exist, and may be used in the construction of Church History.

§ 68. Private Documents include all other writings which can throw light on the history of the Church, and which, in reference to their authority and value as historical materials, may be thrown into three classes.

§ 69. Highest in this respect are contemporary books and papers, whether formally historical, didactic, controversial, practical, devotional, or epistolary, which last are regarded by the best modern writers as peculiarly important, especially when brought to light long after date, and evidently written without any view to publication; so that the very compositions which are most emphatically personal and private often throw most light on public history, by revealing the true sentiments and secret motives of the leading actors, and are therefore gathered up, deciphered, and edited by learned men, with all the critical exactness that was once applied only to the classics or the Scriptures. A remarkable example is DeWette's edition of Luther's letters, with the various readings of the different manuscripts, a work which throws a vivid light on Luther's character and history, as well as on that of the Reformation. A similar effect, though in a less degree, has been produced upon our own revolutionary history, by extracts from inedited or newly-published private correspondence, exhibited in Irving's Life of Washington.

§ 70. Next to these in value, as historical authorities, are works of later date, but made of contemporaneous materials, especially when these are no longer in existence or directly accessible, in which case such works are the only succedaneum, imperfect though it be, for what has thus been lost.

§ 71. The third or residuary class includes all elaborations of historical material, not comprehended under either of the others, that is to say, a large proportion of the historical literature extant.

§ 72. This class, though the lowest in historical authority,—which must not be confounded with literary merit, since the finest modern composition may have less weight as a witness than the most uncouth and ungrammatical contemporary fragment,—has the widest influence upon the general mass of readers, who neither will nor can resort to the original authorities, except by proxy, but for that very reason have the deepest interest in knowing that their proxies are reliable and speak the truth.

§ 73. We are thus brought to the fifth introductory question (*vide supra*, § 1), namely, Who have made use of these materials and brought them into history, and what has been the fruit of their labours?

§ 74. The answer to this question comprises the History, Literature, or Bibliography of Ecclesiastical History.

§ 75. It might have been expected that the early Christian Church would pay great attention to its own history, and bring it to a state of high perfection, as so much attention had been paid to history, both by the classical and sacred writers (§ 45), and the highest models furnished of historiography, as well in Hebrew as in Greek and Latin.

§ 76. But this antecedent probability was so far from being verified by the event, that the first three centuries are almost an entire blank in this respect, few histories having been composed, and of those few none preserved entire.

§ 77. The oldest writer of church history, of whom we have any knowledge, was Hegesippus, a converted Jew of Asia Minor, who, about the middle of the second century, by travelling and otherwise, collected the traditions of the Apostolic Age, now extant only in the shape of fragments and quotations, in the works of later writers.

§ 78. The same may be said of the Chronographia of Julius Africanus, written about a hundred years later.

§ 79. There is no proof that either of these works was a regular historical composition; but, whatever may have been their form or character, they do not seem to have been so much in demand as to secure their preservation, though their disappearance may be owing to causes wholly independent either of their literary merit or the public taste.

§ 80. This remarkable neglect of Ecclesiastical History, in the very period when it might have been expected most to flourish, has been imputed to the constant persecutions of the age; but this is not a satisfactory solution, as they did not hinder other kinds of intellectual exertion; and as some of the interesting historical documents of that age which have been preserved owe both their existence and their subject to these very sufferings; such as the account of the martyrdom of Polycarp, recorded by the church at Smyrna, and that of the persecution in the south of Gaul, by the churches of Lyons and Vienne (§ 498).

§ 81. A better explanation, although still not wholly satisfactory, is, that historical studies were excluded by the general attention to didactic and polemic studies, and especially to philosophical speculation, which, when pushed to an extreme, has always led to the neglect of history.

§ 82. A circumstance which may, at first sight, seem to favour the opinion that persecution was the cause of this neglect is, that the first change for the better took place under Constantine, by whom the church was freed from persecution; but this, if it be more than mere fortuitous coincidence, cannot outweigh the facts just mentioned, as to other forms of intellectual activity.

§ 83. The oldest "Ecclesiastical History," now extant, is the work of Eusebius, bishop of Cesarea, in Palestine, in the early part of the fourth century; the confidential friend and spiritual guide of

Constantine; a man of good mind and considerable learning; of so mild a temper, even towards the erring, as to be suspected of agreement with them; familiarly conversant with all the great events and persons of the day, and deriving great advantages as a historian from his free access to the archives of the empire, as well as to the library founded at Cesarea by his friend Pamphilus, from whom he is sometimes called Eusebius Pamphili.

§ 84. Besides his Preparatio Evangel, which is not so much historical as doctrinal, he wrote a Chronicle and an Ecclesiastical History, to which his account of the martyrs of Palestine, and his panegyrical biography of Constantine, may be regarded as appendices. These works, and especially the Ecclesiastical History, are disfigured by a style at once inflated and jejune, and by a method sometimes wholly arbitrary or fortuitous, and sometimes simply chronological, without any attempt at a digested systematic form. Their chief merits are the personal testimony of a witness so competent and credible to the events of his own time, and the preservation of older documents, fragments and quotations, in a manner which detracts from the literary merit of the composition, but enhances its value as a storehouse of materials.

§ 85. The example of Eusebius was not without effect upon his contemporaries, and especially his followers in the next generation, some of whom wrote history chiefly for polemic purposes; as Epiphanius, to whom we are indebted for most of our knowledge of the ancient heresies; and Philostorgius, whose lost work was intended to maintain the Arian cause. Another lost historian of the fourth century is Sidetes, of Pamphylia, described as a copious, but confused and immethodical, writer.

§ 86. The next century produced several continuators of Eusebius, whose history ends with the year 321; among the rest, two lawyers of Byzantium, Socrates and Sozomen, and an eminent bishop, theologian, and interpreter, Theodoret; all of whom cover nearly the same ground, being a little more than a hundred years.

§ 87. In the beginning of the sixth century, Theodorus, of Constantinople, wrote a continuation of Eusebius, which is lost, and an abridgment, which is extant, but of little value. The last Greek continuator of Eusebius, or of his continuators, is Evagrius of Antioch, about the end of the sixth century, who brought down the history until near that time.

§ 88. The Latin church-historians of the same age were little more than translators and abridgers of the Greeks. The Historia Sacra of the Gallic Presbyter, Sulpicius Severus, called the Christian Sallust, from his comparatively classic style, and the similar work of the Spaniard, Orosius, are universal histories, but contain much religious or ecclesiastical matter. Ruffin or Rufinus, an Italian translated and continued Eusebius. Casiodorus, an Ostrogoth in Italy, by compilation and abridgment, formed a manual, which, with that just mentioned, remained in use as a text-book through the Middle Ages.

§ 89. During the Middle Ages there are no professed church-historians in Greek before Nicephorus Callisti in the thirteenth century; but much ecclesiastical matter is contained in the Byzantine historians (from the end of the fifth to that of the fifteenth century), as the Greek church was not only united with the state, but much involved in politics and court intrigues.

§ 90. The subjugation of the Western Roman Empire (near the end of the fifth century) by the northern barbarians, was followed immediately by great intellectual depression, and remotely by extreme devotion to scholastic studies, which were equally unfriendly to historical and classical pursuits; so that the medieval histories became mere chronicles or annals, among which two of the most celebrated are those of William of Tyre and Matthew Paris, one relating chiefly to the east, the other to the west of Europe.

§ 91. As exceptions to the general dearth of history in the Middle Ages may be mentioned some who wrote the history of their own national churches; such as Gregory of Tours in France, Beda Venerabilis in England, Paulus Deaconus in Italy, and Adam of Bremen in the north of Europe.

§ 92. But besides the literary degradation of church-history in this period, it was morally debased by the increase of superstition, and especially that form of it called Hagiolatry, which led to a rivalry between the tutelary saints of different churches, provinces, and nations, to maintain which their biographies not only usurped the place of more important history, but were first embellished, and then forged, which did not prevent their being sanctioned by ecclesiastical authority, as *legenda*, or lessons to be read in public or private worship, whence our words "legend," "legendary," have become almost synonymous with "fable," "fabulous."

§ 93. The general state of historical knowledge reached its lowest ebb in the age before the Reformation, and was intentionally kept there by the rulers of the church, whose policy it was to represent the existing rites and doctrines as identical with those of the apostolic age; an illusion which would instantly have been dispelled by any clear view of the intervening history.

§ 94. The Revival of Letters, which preceded and prepared the way for the Reformation, or Revival of Religion, gave the first shock to the prevailing ignorance, and by the sceptical criticism of such men as Laurentius Valla, excited a spirit of inquiry into early history as well as doctrine.

§ 95. This spirit of historical inquiry is related to the Reformation, both as a cause and an effect, having led the way to the correction of abuses, and the restoration of a purer faith and practice, which, in their turn, gave a stronger impulse to this class of studies.

§ 96. All the polemic writings of the great

Reformers are so far historical as they demonstrate the corruptions of the Church of Rome to be innovations, and contrast them with the simplicity and purity of ancient times; but Luther and Calvin wrote no formal histories, as their associates and successors, Beza and Melancthon did; a circumstance which seems to show, that the importance of Ecclesiastical History as a means of refuting error, and establishing the truth, was more and more appreciated, as the work of Reformation advanced.

§ 97. The first complete Ecclesiastical History was the product of the Lutheran Reformation, although projected after Luther's death, by one of his most zealous disciples, Matthias Flacius called Illyricus, because a native of the ancient Illyricum, a man of strong mind and great learning, and a strenuous opposer of the Church of Rome, but coarse in taste and violent in temper.

§ 98. To Flacius is due the bold and new conception of a history of the Church upon the largest scale, designed to expose the Romish errors in detail, and trace the progress of corruption from age to age.

§ 99. He had the sagacity to see, that such a work could be successful only in proportion to its fulness and exactness, and to the weight of the authorities on which it rested; as well as that it was beyond the strength of any one man, and could only be accomplished by associated labour.

§ 100. He therefore devised a well-concerted scheme of organization, consisting of five managers or directors (*gubernatores*), and under them ten labourers (*operarii*), seven of whom were to collect materials, two to digest them, and the tenth to write them out.

§ 101. The first part or number of this great work appeared at Basel, from the press of Oporinus, in the year 1559, and the last in January, 1574, under the title of "Historia Ecclesiastica, &c.," but as Flacius and his chief associates were then resident in Magdeburg, and as the centuries were issued seriatim, it has ever since been known by the name of the "Magdeburg Centuries," and its authors as the "Magdeburg Centuriators."

§ 102. This publication acted as a blaze of light upon the darkness of the age, in which the rays which had already been omitted in particular discussions were concentrated and reduced to a complete and regular historical arrangement.

§ 103. At the same time, it raised ecclesiastical history to a position, which it has ever since retained, especially in Germany, and although it repressed for a time the spirit of original investigation, in a field which seemed to be already exhausted, it eventually gave a new and mighty impulse to such studies, in both divisions of the great Protestant body, exciting Lutherans to continue the good work begun among themselves, and stirring up the Calvinists to emulation.

§ 104. Its effect upon the Church of Rome was still more remarkable, as it led, after various attempts to counteract its influence in other ways, to the preparation of a work of the same kind, designed expressly to refute it, and to establish, by historical evidence, the very system which the Centuries were meant to overthrow.

§ 105. The person chosen for this service was a young Dominican of great ability and learning, Cesar Baronius, who was afterwards rewarded for his labours by the dignity of a Cardinal.

§ 106. The "Annals" of Baronius made its first appearance in the year 1588, and was continued by the same hand till the year 1607, the author having access to additional materials contained in the archives of the Papal See, and other repositories inaccessible to Protestants, (*vide supra*,

§ 62); but while this seemed to give him some exclusive advantages, it also tended to excite suspicion in his own church as well as among Protestants, as to the fidelity with which he had made use of these materials, so carefully withheld from public view.

§ 107. The "Annals," although now extremely rare, have been several times reprinted, with and without Renaud's continuation, bringing them down to the latter part of the sixteenth century.

§ 108. These two great works, themselves the fruit of theological discussion in the age of the Reformation, may be represented as the parents of a vast and varied literature, belonging to the province of Ecclesiastical History.

§ 109. Although the Annals of Baronius were intended to maintain the strictest form of Romish doctrine, the later historiography of that church was chiefly in the hands of its more liberal theologians; such as Fra Paolo (Sarpi), the classical and almost Protestant historian of the Council of Trent, to whom Pallavicino bears the same relation as Baronius to the Magdeburg Centuriators.

§ 110. To the same class may be referred a brilliant constellation of historians belonging to the Gallican or Romish church of France, among whom may be named Morinus, Petavius, Tillemont, R. Simon, Fleury, and Natalis Alexander, whose history was composed in such a spirit as to be put upon the Index of forbidden books at Rome.

§ 111. The most elegant and eloquent of these Gallican historians was the famous Bossuet, the most admired preacher and accomplished champion of his church in that age, whose Discourse on Universal History is not only a French classic of the first rank, but a noble view of the whole field from the highest Christian ground, though not without an eye to the exaltation of his own creed and communion.

§ 112. The Reformed or Calvinistic churches of the seventeenth century furnished many zealous and successful rivals of the great historians of the previous age; but it has been noted as a curious fact, that their researches tended rather to special than to general church history, though Hottinger in Switzerland produced a good work of that kind, while Spanheim and the Basnages in Holland, Daillè, Blondel, and Salmasius in France, excelled in cultivating smaller fields.

§ 113. In the same century, the Church of England produced many eminent historical writers, chiefly on special or restricted subjects, among whom may be named as representatives, Archbishop Usher; Bishops Pearson, Beveridge, and Burnet; Doctors Dodwell, Cave, Bull, and Bingham, who is still one of the highest authorities in the department of Ecclesiastical Antiquities, or Christian Archæology (*vide supra*, § 43).

§ 114. The tone of church history continued to be controversial or polemic, more especially in Germany, until Calixtus, in the seventeenth century, attempted to introduce a more pacific and dispassionate mode of treating the subject, with a view to the promotion of his favourite scheme of reuniting all Christian churches, on the doctrinal and ecclesiastical basis of the first six centuries; but the unpopularity of this scheme gave him little influence on contemporary historiography.

§ 115. More success, in this direction, attended the efforts of Spener, the first founder of the Pietists, to moderate polemic rancour, and to make experimental piety the essence of church history, as well as of Christianity itself; while the orthodox Lutherans of the same date, like the Calvinistic writers of an earlier day, spent their strength chiefly upon special subjects, such as the History of the Reformation, as composed by Seckendorf and others.

§ 116. This new mode of writing history was pushed to an extreme by Godfrey Arnold, in the early part of the last century, who allowed his feelings as a Pietist, and therefore an opponent of the Orthodox Lutherans, to govern him so far, that he espoused the cause of heretics in general, and, without embracing their opinions, undertook to show that they were often, if not always, morally in the right, and the Church, as a body, in the wrong. This work, although it gave rise to a long and angry controversy, was deprived of permanent and popular effect by its paradoxical character and by its harsh and unattractive style.

§ 117. Though Arnold, strictly speaking, had no follower, his very excesses, when contrasted with those of previous writers in the opposite direction, contributed still further to divest Ecclesiastical History of its predominant polemic tone, and to promote a more impartial and dispassionate treatment of the subject; as appears from the tone of the most eminent historians in the first half of the eighteenth century, as well among the Lutherans (such as Buddeus, Fabricius, and Weismann) as among the Calvinists (such as Jablonski, Venema, J. A. Turretin, Lenfant, Beausobre and Le Clerc, or Clericus); and the same thing is measurably true of Romish writers also (such as Orsi and Mansi).

§ 118. The danger now was that the controversial spirit would give place to one of cold indifference as to matters in dispute, even where the writer really adhered to orthodox opinions; and this fear is thought by some to have been realized in the case of the next distinguished writer, who exerted a commanding influence both on contemporaneous and on subsequent historiography, John Laurence Mosheim, who died in 1755, after holding a conspicuous position during many years, at Helmstadt and Göttingen.

§ 119. Besides a multitude of books and tracts on various subjects, chiefly belonging to Church History, he published two, which have never lost their place among the highest secondary or derivative authorities (see § 71); his "Commentaries on the State of Christianity before the time of Constantine," and his "Institutes of Ecclesiastical History, Ancient and Modern;" both which have been translated into English, and the last of which, though now comparatively little used in Germany, has long been a favourite text-book, both in England and America.

§ 120. The works of Mosheim are distinguished, in addition to the absence of all warmth and passion, by a thorough knowledge of the subject, rare acuteness and sagacity in critical conjecture and historical combination; great completeness and exactness as to the essential facts of history; extreme formality and clearness of arrangement, and especially by classical elegance of Latin style, which last attraction is of course wanting, both in the free or rather loose translation of Maclaine, and in the accurate but awkward one of Murdock, who has added to the value of the original, considered as a storehouse of facts, but not to its beauty as a composition by his numerous and often overloaded notes.

§ 121. The influence of Mosheim's better taste and temper may be traced in the German writers who succeeded him, among whom may be named as representatives, Baumgarten, Cramer, Pfaff, and the two Walchs, father and son, several of whom, as well as others not here mentioned, have independent merits of their own.

§ 122. The next important change in historical

writing and investigation was occasioned by the rise of German rationalism or neology, of which the reputed father is John Solomon Semler, professor at Halle, who, although educated in the strictest forms of Pietism, and never wholly emancipated from its influence, did more perhaps than any other person to shake the foundations of men's faith in the divine authority of Scripture, by calling every thing in question, and suggesting doubts as to the authenticity of almost every book in the Bible, a sceptical criticism which has been carried to still greater length by later writers, in reference both to Scripture and Church History, to which it was applied by Semler himself, not in regular historical compositions, but in various confused, ill-written works, and, still more, through the intermediate agency of pupils and disciples.

§ 123. The sceptical tendency thus introduced into the study of Church History had very different effects on different classes; in frivolous and shallow minds engendering contempt for the whole subject, and producing works of a satirical and scoffing tone, such as those of Spittler and Henke; while in minds of greater depth and earnestness, even when destitute of strong faith in the truth of Christianity, it led to a laborious reconstruction of Church History by working up the original materials afresh, and giving them a new shape, either in general works (such as the gigantic one of Schröckh), or special treatises (like those of Planek and Stäudlin).

§ 124. To the latter class belongs an extensive literature of recent date, beginning near the close of the last century, and flourishing especially during the first quarter of the present, being one of the good, incidental fruits of the new impulse given to historical research by the sceptical or rationalistic movement, which produced a strong taste and demand for monographs, or thorough and minute investigations of some single doctrine, period, or personage, derived directly from original authorities, and published as a separate and independent work.

§ 125. Besides the interest imparted to many distinct topics of Church History by this detailed and thorough mode of treating them, these monographs were gradually storing up materials for new works of a general and comprehensive character, to fill the chasms or supply the place of those which had appeared before these new researches and accumulations were begun; the very same persons sometimes taking part in both the processes, that is, distinguishing themselves as writers both of monographs and general church histories.

§ 126. The most signal instance of this twofold labour and success is that afforded by Neander, of Jewish birth, but Christian education, a child in spirit and in secular affairs, but in intellect a man, and in learning a giant, for many years an eminent professor at Berlin, where he died in 1850, and now acknowledged to have no superior as a general writer on Church History, but first distinguished, in his early manhood, as the author of invaluable monographs or special treatises on Julian the Apostate, on Tertullian, on Chrysostom, and on Bernard, each of which, besides a full biography, including a large portion of contemporary history, contains a critical analysis of many ancient and important works.

§ 127. At the close of the first quarter of the nineteenth century, the time seemed to be come for the reduction of these new or freshly gathered stores to a complete and systematic whole in general church histories; a crisis indicated by the almost simultaneous commencement of two great works which are still unfinished, but unanimously reckoned, by all competent authorities, to be the two great master-pieces of the age in this department, one by Neander, which appeared in 1825, and the other in the preceding year, by Gieseler, who was already known as a learned and sagacious critic, one of his ablest compositions being a review of Neander's Tertullian, in which he developed his own theory of Gnosticism.

§ 128. The authors of these two works are as much alike in some points as they are unlike in others, the resemblance lying in their education and extent of reading, their official positions and professional employments, their integrity and truthfulness, and their use, for the most part, of the same materials, both being thoroughly and equally familiar with the oldest authorities, and the freshest forms into which the raw material had been newly wrought; the difference lying in the calm impartiality of Gieseler as contrasted with the honest and enlightened zeal of Neander; and in the moderate and unimpassioned rationalism of the one, compared with the warm but meagre Christianity of the other.

§ 129. The books themselves are as unlike as their authors, both in plan and execution; Gieseler's consisting of an exquisite selection from the very words of the original authorities, arranged as notes and strung together by a slender thread of narrative; Neander's of the very same materials, but digested in his own mind, and wrought up into a flowing homogeneous narrative, exhibiting the express of his character in almost every page and sentence; the one as perfectly objective as the other is subjective in its whole design and structure; the one enabling every reader to construct the history for himself, the other exhibiting it ready-made, but by the hand of a master.

§. 130. The difference just mentioned may account for the fact that Gieseler, although universally applauded, and implicitly relied upon for facts and for materials, has founded no distinct school, and propagated no peculiar mode of writing history; whereas Neander has had many professed followers, who hold his principles, adopt his plans, and sometimes even imitate his style and manner.

§ 131. Among the most faithful and yet most independent followers of Neander may be mentioned Guericke, who carries out his master's plan in a more compendious form, but with an almost bigoted attachment to the peculiar doctrines of Luther, and in a style so crabbed and involved as to forbid translation or convenient use in elementary instruction, although it has been eminently useful as a vehicle, not only of the best historical knowledge, but of sincere piety and sound religious principles in all essential points.

§ 132. Another representative of this school is Jacobi, less orthodox and pious than Guericke, but nearer to Neander in sentiment and spirit, and superior to both in clearness and simplicity of style and method, which, together with the fact that his work was suggested and commended to the public by Neander, as the best compendious view of his own system, although far from being a mere abridgment, makes it matter of regret that it has not yet gone beyond a single part or volume, extending not quite to the close of the sixth century.

§ 133. As other offshoots of Neander's stock, though very different, in some points, both from him and from each other, may be named Schaff of Mercerburg and Lange of Zurich; but as neither of these writers has yet brought his work below the Apostolic age, they can scarcely be considered as belonging to our present subject.

§ 134. Still more unlike Neander, both in sentiment and method, although evidently nurtured in his school, is Hase of Jena, a man of genius and of cultivated taste, and an original and brilliant writer, but unduly partial to the mere æsthetic and artistical relations of his subject, not so much a believer as an admirer of the Gospel (rather than a believer), and so often obscure from epigrammatic or laconic brevity, and from rather presupposing than detailing facts, that he is scarcely more translatable or fit for elementary instruction than Guericke himself, though otherwise no two writers can be more dissimilar and even opposite.

§ 135. One of the latest and best German writers is John Henry Kurtz, now Professor at Dorpat, but for many years a Gymnasial teacher, which has given him a practical acquaintance with the wants of students, while his thorough knowledge of the Biblical History, on which he is the author of some admirable works, gives him a great advantage over some justly celebrated church historians. His facility and zeal as a maker of books have tempted him to vary their form and multiply their number to excess; but all of them are sound, clear, wholesome in tendency, and admirably suited both to academical and general use.

§ 136. One of the most singular effects of modern German changes in this science is the frequent adoption of the form and method common among Protestants, by Roman Catholic historians, including liberality of tone and abstinence from all polemic violence, but really by that means tending to insinuate their own views more effectually into the minds of unsuspicious readers; while in Italy, and even in France, works of this class still retain the bigoted exclusive form, by which they have always been distinguished from the writings of Reformed theologians. Of the former, Alzog's "Universal History of the Christian Church" may be taken as a sample; of the latter, S. L'Homond's "History of the Church," as re-written by the Abbe Postel, for the use of schools and families in France.

§ 137. In the British isles, Ecclesiastical History has been chiefly cultivated in the Church of England and the great Universities of Oxford and Cambridge, or by men instructed there, of late years more or less controlled by German influence, but never without much independent use of the original authorities, and almost always with the rare advantage of general culture, classical scholarship, and a native English style.

§ 138. Near the end of the last century, Joseph Milner, an Anglican clergyman of the evangelical or low-church party, and a man of greater piety and learning than sound judgment, wrote the history of the church until the Reformation, with the avowed purpose of making practical religion or experimental Christianity the great subject of his work, and passing over all that does not bear upon it, a plan injudicious in itself, and very imperfect in its execution, doing credit to the author's own religious character and sentiments, and generally edifying to 'the' readers of congenial spirit, but, as might have been expected, partial and onesided, and exceedingly imperfect as a full view of the whole subject.

§ 139. Milman, now the Dean of St. Paul's, London, previously well known as a poet, an historian of the Jews, and an editor of Gibbon, has also written a "History of Christianity to the abolition of Paganism in the Roman Empire," since continued in his "History of Latin Christianity," extending to Nicolas V., a work distinguished by originality and erudition, an elegant though not an easy style, and free to a great extent from that apparent sympathy with German scepticism or latitudinarianism, with which some of his earlier works had been reproached, but not entitled to the praise of having carried Church History beyond the point where Gieseler and Neander left it.

§ 140. Equally scholarlike and elegant, and still more Christian in their tone, but at the same time still more Anglican in sentiment and prepossession, although free from any thing offensive in pretension or assumption, are the "History of the Christian Church to the Pontificate of Gregory the

Great," by J. C. Robertson, a beneficed clergyman in England, and the "History of the Christian Church during the first three centuries," by J. J. Blunt, late Professor of Divinity at Cambridge, the latter a posthumous collection of the Author's Academical Lectures; the former intended for the use of general readers, as well as of students in theology

§ 141. One of the latest and best English works of this class is the "History of the Christian Church during the Middle Age, and during the Reformation," by the Rev. Charles Hardwick, formerly of Cambridge, then of Harrow, now of King's College, London, the two volumes forming part of a Series of Theological Manuals, for the use of candidates for orders in the Church of England, prepared by several different writers, and now issuing at Cambridge. The two in question show an intimate acquaintance with the modern German literature, as well as the original authorities, soundness on all essential doctrines, avowed attachment to the polity and worship of the author's church, but scrupulous courtesy and candor towards others, with a clearness of method, elegance of style, and beauty of typography not often found in combination.

§ 142. None of these modern English writers on Church History, betray the slightest tendency or tenderness towards Romish error, such as may be traced in the "Ecclesiastical History" of Palmer, one of the Oxford Theologians, republished in America by Bp. Whittingham, of Maryland, and adapted to parochial instruction. This work, which is a small and slight one, without any pretension to original or independent value, is the only general Church History with which I am acquainted, representing or proceeding from the Puseyite or Romish party in the Church of Engand.

§ 143. The sixth and last introductory topic is that of method, involving two questions, what method has been pursued by the best writers, and what method shall we adopt ourselves; the answer to the second depending in some measure on the answer to the first, as we may profit by the failures as well as the successes of our predecessors, without any annoyance on our part, since by standing on the shoulders of a giant, even a pigmy may see further.

§ 144. By *method* is here meant such a distribution or arrangement of a subject as is neither *accidental*, i. e. determined by causes independent of the writer's will and judgment; nor *arbitrary*,

i. e. determined by his will alone; but *rational*, i. e. determined by an act of judgment, and for which a reason can be given.

§ 145. Method is essential to all science, even in the widest sense, because it enters into the very definition or idea of science, as rational or systematic knowledge; but is especially important in those sciences which do not rest on demonstration, mathematical or moral, and which do not therefore dictate their own method, as geometry and logic do.

§ 146. The choice of a good method is especially important in historical studies, because there are so many ways in which the same facts may be stated, without any variation from substantial truth, as appears, not only from the usages of historical composition, but also from the usages of common life, no two men commonly adopting the same form or order in relating the most trivial incident.

§ 147. But while this makes the choice of a good method indispensable in all history, there is nothing in the nature of Ecclesiastical History in particular, requiring a method wholly peculiar to itself, by assuming which necessity, historians of the church have not only hindered the progress of their readers, but gratuitously planted a great gulf between this part of history and every other.

§ 148. The rudest and crudest form of historical composition is the anecdotic; in which the materials are arranged at random, or as they come to the historian's knowledge, or occur to his mind in the act of writing.

§ 149. The first step towards a rational method is the chronological arrangement of events in the order of their occurrence, which distinguishes chronicles or annals, both from anecdotes on one hand, and from history properly so called upon the other.

§ 150. But this step, though essential, is not sufficient of itself, since it does not bring together things which belong together, or have an affinity arising from their very nature; and yet this is the very end of method.

§ 151. The next step towards a rational method is the topical arrangement, or the combination of things mutually similar or akin, whether contemporaneous and successive or not.

§ 152. But neither is this sufficient of itself without regard to chronological order, because this order is essential to history, and if neglected, the materials, however well arranged as topics, become wholly confused, or lose their historical character and bearing.

§ 153. These two methods therefore—and there seems to be no other not reducible to these—are both essential, not apart but together, and must be combined in order to produce a history; and as this combination may exist in different proportions and be exhibited in various shapes, it still remains a question how it may be best effected.

§ 154. In answering this question, great use may be made of previous experience, or the history of the efforts which have been made to solve this problem. (See § 143.)

§ 155. In tracing this history, however, we need not go very far back, since the use of method, properly so called *in Ecclesiastical History*, is a matter of comparatively recent date.

§ 156. The ancient writers of Ecclesiastical History seldom rise above the simple chronological arrangement, and are often wholly arbitrary or fortuitous in their arrangement, as may be seen from the example of Eusebius and his followers.

§ 157. The first genuine attempt at the solution

of this problem was made by the Magdeburg Centuriators, who exhibit for the first time, a combined chronological and topical arrangement on the largest scale. (See §§ 97–101.)

§ 158. The chronical arrangement of this great work is by centuries, for which the singular reason is assigned, that there is really a cycle or complete revolution of events in every hundred years; a theory never, perhaps, generally current, or long since exploded.

§ 159. The topical arrangement under each century consists of fifteen heads or rubrics, with a prefatory summary or general view, making sixteen in all—viz.: 1. General view. 2. Extent of the church. 3. Its external condition. 4. Doctrines. 5. Heresies. 6. Rites. 7. Polity. 8. Schisms. 9. Councils. 10. Bishops and Doctors. 11. Heretics. 12. Martyrs. 13. Miracles. 14. Jews. 15. Other religions. 16. Political changes affecting the condition of the church.

§ 160. The fourth category, that of doctrine, is subdivided into more than fifty heads, the mere titles of which fill eleven folio columns, and constitute the framework of a body of divinity, as full and methodical as that of Tertullian.

§ 161. The extent and minuteness of this topic shows or confirms, what is certain otherwise, that the immediate purpose of this great work was polemical or controversial; to promote which, great minuteness of specification was required, in order to assail the Church of Rome at as many salient points as possible.

§ 162. It appears from the preface or prospectus of the work, prefixed to the first Century, that the method was not framed by induction from a detailed survey of the materials, but constructed *a priori*, as a framework, in or under which the materials, when collected, were to be digested.

§ 163. It appears from the same preface, and from an inspection of the work itself, that this provisional arrangement was originally framed with reference to the early centuries, though afterwards extended, for the sake of uniformity, to all the others, without any change whatever, so that under each, down to the thirteenth, we find the rubric of miracles long after they had ceased, and that of martyrs when there were no persecutions, except so far as the historians were tempted to admit factitious or imaginary miracles and martyrs, for the very sake of filling up their pigeon-holes or niches.

§ 164. The three facts stated in the last three paragraphs suffice to show that the arrangement of the Centuries, though admirably suited to a temporary purpose, was neither suited nor intended to be made perpetual, but is expressly represented by its authors as a first draught in an untried field, admitting and requiring subsequent amendment.

§ 165. And yet this cumbersome and complicated system has given character to subsequent historiography, especially in Germany, the later changes being not of principle, but form, and all contributing together to give this part of history a character peculiar to itself, and to divorce it from all others.

§ 166. The real merit of the plan of the Centuriators is its adaptation to its immediate purpose, and its convenience, even now, as a book of reference in polemic theology, arising from the fulness and minuteness of its subdivisions, aided by a very complete index to each Century.

§ 167. But however useful when referred to as a dictionary, it was made almost useless as a book to be continuously read, by the very circumstances just referred to, and by the dispersion of facts belonging to the same subject under different and distant heads; e. g. the history of an important heresy might be divided between No. 4 (doctrine), No. 5 (heresies), No. 8 (schisms), No. 9 (councils), No. 10 (bishops and doctors), No. 11 (heretics), and No. 15 (civil or political events, which would include the action of the government in all its changes).

§ 168. The influence of this great work on method was naturally less in other churches, and we find accordingly some Romish writers adopting a much simpler plan, such as the biographical arrangement of Tillemont, who groups all incidents, as far as possible, around certain names or persons; an arrangement highly useful in imparting life and individual interest to dry details, and, therefore, often revived since, among the rest, by Rudelbach and Böhringer of late years, but defective as a form of general history, because some topics cannot be reduced to it without an artificial violence, sufficient to condemn it as an aid to the understanding or the memory.

§ 169. But besides these foreign variations, changes became necessary in the mode of treating Ecclesiastical History, even in Germany, and in the Lutheran church, required by the gradual decline of the old controversial spirit, or rather by the new forms in which it revealed itself, as well as by a gradual change, if not improvement, in the public taste.

§ 170. This change of method was almost insensible, and spread through many generations, but may be said to have attained its first development and elimination in the Institutiones of Mosheim. (See §§ 118–120).

§ 171. This change, however, though apparently so great, is not so much a change of principle as of detail and outward form, consisting in the simplification of what was complex, and the embellishment of what was rugged and uncouth, without departing from the essential features of the older methods.

§ 172. He retains the centurial arrangement, not as founded in the nature of things (see § 158), but as commonly preferred and universally familiar, and improves it by distributing the centuries in four groups, which may be regarded as the form of the modern periodologies.

§ 173. In his topical method he retains the rubrical arrangement, but reduces the number of divisions, and adopts a more symmetrical adjustment, throwing the whole under the two heads of External and Internal History, dividing the former into

Prosperous and Adverse changes; the first including all additions to the area of Christianity, and friendly relations to the state and to society; the latter all contractions of the field by conquest, persecution, or apostasy; while under the internal head he groups, 1st, the history of learning, education, and philosophy; 2d, Church government and teachers; 3d, theology, didactic, biblical, polemic, moral; 4th, rites and ceremonies; 5th, heresies and schisms.

§ 174. That this is really the old Magdeburg method, in a somewhat improved shape, is evident not only from its very form, but from its practical effects, as we still have heresies and heretics, doctrine and doctors, theologians and theology, divided from each other in a very artificial inconvenient manner, so that the author is compelled in some parts of his work to abandon his own method as unmanageable, even by himself.

§ 175. It was not to be expected that the new impulse given to historical inquiry by the sceptical criticism (§§ 122–124), would leave the method of ecclesiastical historiography unchanged; and accordingly we find new methods multiplying very fast within the last half century.

§ 176. But what is truly strange is that the

Germans, even in the act of making all things new, should have retained the rubrical arrangement, at least in its essential principle, and made a thorough change only in the chronological arrangement of the subject.

§ 177. This change consists in discarding the centurial arrangement altogether, as a framework of the history, and substituting periods of unequal length, determined by important points or epochs, without any reference to the centuries at all.

§ 178. The only change in the topical arrangement is a formal one, consisting in a further improvement upon Mosheim's plan in point of clearness and simplicity, and the reduction of the heads to the smallest possible number that can be reconciled with the rubrical principle at all, which principle is still retained and rigorously carried out.

§ 179. These modern methods vary from each other in detail, but the essential type is that afforded by Neander, who reduces all the topics to four heads or classes: 1. The enlargement and contraction of the area of Christendom, including its relations to the state and to society. 2. Its organization, government, and discipline. 3. Its doctrines, controversies, heresies, and theologians. 4.

Christian life, including worship, with its rites and forms, and practical religion as exemplified in the lives of its professors. The most important topic added by some modern church historians is that of Art as auxiliary to religion, including Poetry, Music, Architecture, Painting, and Sculpture, so far as they have been enlisted in the service of the church.

§ 180. This latest form of ecclesiastical historiography appears to be regarded as the ultimatum of improvement, not only by the Germans who invented it, but by their imitators and disciples elsewhere, who sometimes apologize for using a less scientific and more popular arrangement, like that employed in secular or general history; as if this resemblance were a necessary evil, and not the greatest possible advantage, and the strongest recommendation of the method which exhibits it. (Quote as an example the last paragraph of Robertson's preface.)

§ 181. It may, therefore, seem presumptuous, without any such apology, to question the perfection of this modern and fashionable system, so far as it is really a new one, by objecting, not (only) to its details, but to its principle, and more especially to its beginning at the wrong end in its process of improvement, retaining the rubrical arrangement notwithstanding its acknowledged inconveniences, and making a thorough alteration only in the chronical arrangement, which was far less objectionable and defective.

§ 182. The objection made by this school to the old centurial arrangement is that it is arbitrary and mechanical; a singular contrast to the doctrine of the Magdeburg Centuriators, who supposed it to be founded in the nature of the subject and the providential laws which govern the succession of events (§ 158), a doctrine which however was abandoned (if it ever had been current) by, or before, Mosheim. (§ 172.)

§ 183. The fact alleged may be admitted, but with two qualifications, which materially influence its force as an objection; first, that as all chronological divisions are expedients to assist the memory, not arising necessarily from something in the nature of the subject, but the fruit of "art and man's device;" however rational and well-contrived, their being contrived at all subjects them to the charge of being arbitrary, and to some degree mechanical or formal.

§ 184. The second qualifying circumstance is

really included in the first, but may be separately stated, namely, that the same charge lies against the very methods of division and arrangement which it is proposed to substitute for the centurial; since every periodology that has ever been proposed is, after all, an artificial framework, which requires some effort of the understanding to insert it in its proper place, and still more effort of the memory to keep it there.

§ 185. Sometimes this vague charge is made more specific, by alleging that the centurial arrangement absurdly presupposes all the various series of events, and sequences of causes and effects, to be simultaneuosly wound up at the end of every hundred years; whereas the threads are of unequal length, and while one falls short of the century another overruns into the next.

§ 186. But besides the false reproach thus cast upon the old arrangement, which (except in the case of the Magdeburg Centuriators) purports to be only an approximation and a practical convenience (§§ 172–182), this plausible objection quietly ignores the fact, that the very same thing may be said with equal truth, though not true to the same extent, of every periodical arrangement that can be imagined; for, however nearly such divisions may approach to the ideal standard, it will not be seriously alleged that any of them has succeeded in making all the threads of history coincident in their commencement and their termination, so that nothing overruns the mark or falls short of it.

§ 187. That this is peculiarly the case with the centuries, as being more numerous and uniform, is true; but this difference of degree may be outweighed by peculiar advantages of other kinds; such as perfect uniformity of length, requiring no repeated effort of the understanding or the memory to retain or to recall them; and their universal use, not only making them still more familiar, but maintaining the connection between this and other kinds of history, which all peculiar methods tend to weaken and destroy.

§ 188. Another qualifying circumstance in favour of the old arrangement is, that even those who are most zealous for the Periods, and against the Centuries, are after all obliged to make the latter the substratum of their own plans, not only by referring particular events to such and such a century, but by ascribing to whole centuries, as such, a definite distinctive character; so that instead of superseding the old method by a new and better one, they often spoil both by confounding and entangling them together.

§ 189. All this would be true if the modern German school had succeeded in uniting upon some one scheme or system of great periods to supersede the centuries; but how much more when the results are so endlessly diversified, that there seems ground to fear that the process of invention will defeat itself, by making all points salient and every notable event an epoch.

§ 190. Nor is it merely the diversity and number of the modern periodical arrangements that detracts from their utility, but also their exclusive character, when made the framework of a general church history; in consequence of which, he who follows Gieseler's method cannot make use of Neander's, even in the way of reference, without trouble and confusion, since the same event which stands at the beginning of a period in one, may stand at the conclusion of a different period in another; to say nothing of the general dislocation and distortion which result from the comparison or simultaneous use of methods so unlike and so exclusive of each other.

§ 191. While these objections may be made to

the entire change introduced into the chronical arrangement of Church History by the modern German school, there are others, of a very different nature, to the partial change effected in the topical or rubrical arrangement, over and above the general objection which has been already stated (§ 181), that it is a partial change and not a total one.

§ 192. The essence of the rubrical arrangement, common to the earliest and latest German church-historians, is the practice of pursuing every topic, whether there be few or many, through the whole of every period, whether long or short, and then beginning with the next until the schedule is completed, the divisions and the titles being absolutely uniform in every case.

§ 193. To this essential feature of the system invented by the Magdeburg Centuriators, and adhered to even by their harshest critics, notwithstanding endless variations in detail, and vast improvements in simplicity and symmetry of form, there are various objections, which may however be reduced to three, drawn from History, Analogy, and Experience.

§ 194. The historical objection to the rubrical arrangement, as above described (§ 192), is that it originated with the Magdeburg Centuriators, and was generated in the violent polemic fermentations of that age, a genesis which raises a presumption adverse to its permanent utility, since every age must have its own mode of assailing error and defending truth, even when the truth and error are unchanged, and since the world has long ceased to regard Church History as a mere offensive weapon or defensive armour in religious warfare.

§ 195. If this objection be well founded, the mere formal changes which have been made in the rubrical arrangement, however valuable in themselves or in relation to some other standard, do not remove the ground of the objection, since an increase of simplicity and symmetry detracts from the original efficiency of this contrivance, which arose in a large measure from the very features which are thus removed, without relieving its defects and inconveniences, considered as a means to other ends.

§ 196. But as the origin of this plan could afford no good reason for condemning and rejecting it, if in itself good, an additional objection may be drawn from the analogy of history and historiography in general, to wit, that the method now in question is peculiar to Church History (except so far as its example affected the practice of the secular historians), having never been found necessary or expedient by historians of any other class or period, ancient or modern, sacred or profane; a circumstance not only very strong, as a presumptive proof, at least, that it is equally unnecessary elsewhere, but a key to the otherwise inexplicable difference of form and method, between this one kind of history and every other. (§ 147.)

§ 197. Even this peculiarity of form, however, would be quite as insufficient as its mere historical extraction, to condemn the method, if it were not open to the practical objection, that instead of exciting greater interest in this important study, it has seemed to make it less attractive, and instead of aiding the memory, which some have made a reason for adopting it, has tantalized and weakened it, by endless repetition of the same monotonous and lifeless forms under which the actual variety of history is lost or hidden, like soldiers in a uniform, or mummers in a masquerade.

§ 198. One fact may be considered certain, however it may be explained, to wit, that no such method, or at least no such extensive and detailed application of it, would be tolerated in any field of history where a less artificial arrangement has become familiar; as, for instance, in the history of the American and French Revolutions, or, what is nearly the same thing, the lives of Washington and Bonaparte, in writing which, although the materials are so abundant and the phases or aspects of the subject so diversified, the thought of dividing the whole matter into periods, and then going through or over each in several successive journeys, first collecting all the military facts, then the political, and then the personal or private, has happily never occurred to any of the eminent historians, by whom these two great themes have been successively handled, from Marshall to Irving, and from Scott to Thiers.

§ 199. On the strength of these considerations, drawn from history, analogy, and practical effects, it may not be unlawful, after all, to attempt another movement in advance, by improving, if possible, on both parts of the method now in vogue, to wit, its Chronological and Topical arrangement; especially as this change is proposed, at least in the first instance, only as a limited experiment, confined, both in its good and bad effects, to the classes of a single institution, and indeed to the instructions of a single teacher.

§ 200. With respect to the Topical part of the

system, the proposed change is to set aside the rubrical arrangement altogether, as a framework running through the history and determining its whole form, and to substitute a natural arrangement of the topics, by combining a general chronological order with a due regard to the mutual relative importance of the topics themselves; so that what is prominent at one time may be wholly in the background at another, instead of giving all an equal prominence at all times, by applying the same scheme or formula to all alike.

§ 201. This natural method, so called to distinguish it from every artificial or conventional arrangement, far from being new, is recommended by the practice and example of the best historians in every language and in every age; affording a presumptive, if not a conclusive, proof both of its theoretical consistency and of its practical efficiency and usefulness, and at the same time a convenient means of keeping this and other parts of universal history in mutual connection and agreement with each other.

§ 202. With respect to the Chronical division and arrangement, the change proposed is neither to add one more to the exclusive schemes already extant, nor to retain any one of them exclusively of all the rest, but simply to avail ourselves of all of them, so far as they can be combined, both as intrinsically valuable aids in historical study, and as a means of making all the most important systems of Church History alike and simultaneously available.

§ 203. In order to accomplish this design, the chronological arrangement must be, as far as possible, separated from topical details; so that instead of two conflicting methods crossing each other, and dividing the whole subject upon different and often inconsistent principles, there may be still two methods, and the same two, but distinctly and successively presented, not promiscuously mingled, both in the foundation and the superstructure of the history, considered as a building, but the one (the chronological division) underlying the other (the topical division), as a basis underlies the superstructure; or, to use another architectural analogy, the one affording, as a framework, both the space and the form into which the other, as material, is to be arranged and built.

§ 204. This idea can be realized, if realized at all, only by taking two successive views or surveys of the whole field; one more general, the other more particular; one conducted on a chronical, the other on a topical arrangement; or in other words, by making the chronological division of the subject introductory, and prior to the topical details, which may then be treated in the form and order which experience may indicate as most convenient, without any subdivision or restriction, except such as may be suggested by the nature, or the subject, or the taste and inclination of the writer.

§ 205. The two modes of division and arrangement being thus retained, but sundered, we obtain not only an exemption from the irksome and injurious necessity of breaking off in the examination of a topic because some imaginary line is reached, and must not be overleaped till every other topic has been brought up to the same mark, but also the opportunity of placing side by side as many chronological arrangements as we please, not only to compare them once for all, but to retain them and employ them, both as aids in the study of the subject, and as keys to the respective systems which they represent, and of which they are constituent elements or component parts.

§ 206. The difference between the method here proposed, and that which it is meant to supersede, may be illustrated by the actual division of a literal field or tract of land by a system of walls and ditches, which of course excludes every other system of the same kind, since the combination of the two, and still more of many, would cut up the supposed field into irregular and useless parts; whereas any number of such systems may be drawn on paper, or even marked upon the surface of the ground, without interference or collision, and perhaps with great facilities of mutual comparison and combination.

§ 207. It is proposed then to divide the course of history before us into two unequal parts, the first and lesser part consisting of a general survey of the whole field, and of the various ways in which it has been or may be divided and subdivided, distributed and arranged, for the purpose of a more detailed examination; the second and larger part containing this detailed examination itself, in the natural order of its topics, unrestricted by the previous chronological divisions, but with all the advantage of assuming and referring to them, as a means of fixing dates, and of comparing the positions occupied by any given topic or event in different schemes or systems of Church History.

§ 208. The first of these surveys, although the least thorough and extensive, derives great relative importance from the use which we propose to make of it, as the foundation or the framework of the other, the completeness and success of which must therefore be dependent, in a great degree, upon the clearness and precision of this introductory and general view.

§ 209. The confusion and complexity which must arise from an attempt to look at various periodologies at once, may be avoided by surveying them successively and *seriatim*, just as the face of any country may be studied, with the aid of skeleton or outline maps, by confining the attention first to one physical feature, such as mountains, with the natural divisions which they form or mark out, then proceeding to another, such as streams and water-courses; then superadding the political distinctions and designations; or as one previously familiar with all these, may use a railway map of the same region without difficulty or confusion.

§ 210. But in order to pursue this gradual process with advantage, it is important to begin right, i. e. not with what is complex and obscure, which would defeat the end at once, but with that which is comparatively simple, i. e. exhibiting the smallest number of dividing lines and consequent divisions, so that from these we may proceed almost insensibly to those of a more minute and complex character.

§ 211. Another most desirable condition, if attainable, in such a primary division of the subject, is that it be not only simple in itself, but familiar from extensive use and general application.

§ 212. If these two qualities could only be had separately and apart, it might be hard to choose between a simple method little known, and one more complex but extensively familiar.

§ 213. By a happy coincidence, however, both conditions may be said to meet in one mode of arranging and distributing Church History, to wit, the division into three great periods, the Ancient, Middle, and Modern Ages.

§ 214. The simplicity of this mode speaks for itself, while its previous and general familiarity appears in the first instance, from its use in common parlance and in general usage, which have few expressions more familiar than that of "Middle Ages," implying both the others; and then from its adoption by all modern church historians, either tacitly and indirectly, as by Mosheim, Gieseler, and Neander, or avowedly and formally, as by Guericke, Hase, [Niedner], Kurtz, and Schaff.

§ 215. The reality and usefulness of these divisions are entirely independent of precision in their boundaries; as the latter may be variable and doubtful, while the former are self-evident and palpable; just as a surveyor, before running a line or measuring a foot, may obtain, from an elevated point in the tract to be surveyed, a perfectly distinct impression of its principal features,—water, woodland, meadow, tillage,—not only in themselves, but in their relative position and general comparative extent; or as the student of ancient geography may learn as much as can be known, or need be known, as to the relative position of the tribes of Israel, and the states of Greece, without any bounding lines at all, which can only be assigned by guess; as the modern geographer or politician readily distinguishes between the northern, eastern, middle, southern, western States of the American Union, though the lines of demarcation may be variously drawn; as no man doubts the real difference between childhood, youth, maturity, and old age; or between morning, evening, twilight, night; or between the seasons of the year; although he cannot positively draw the line or fix the point where any one of these divisions ceases and the next begins.

§ 216. The conclusion to be drawn from these

analogies is, that even if we were without any definite boundaries whatever between these three great divisions of the field of history, the divisions themselves might be distinctly marked and usefully employed, the difference lying not in the edges, but the central map, or rather in the whole extent, as the prismatic colours of the rainbow may be perfectly distinguishable, although they appear to fade into each other by a vanishing and almost imperceptible transition.

§ 217. The case however is not really so bad as we have here assumed, there being a tolerably well defined limit, especially between the Middle Ages and the Modern, which are universally agreed to be divided by the Reformation, excepting only some extreme ultramontane Papists, such as Postel (§ 136), who makes the Reformation a mere subdivision in one of his great periods, extending from the fall of the Greek Empire to the close of the Council of Trent. (§ 317.)

§ 218. There is less unanimity in reference to the boundary between the First and Middle Ages, because the transition there is not effected by a great revolution (religious, intellectual, and social), which is always definite in date, because sudden in its outbreak, however long its causes may have been in operation; but by a plurality of changes which reached their height, or attained maturity at different, although not at distant, points of time, just as different fruits ripen in succession, and yet all belong to the same season; so that by making one or another of these changes prominent, we gain a somewhat different line of demarcation.

§ 219. Although, for reasons which have just been stated (§§ 215, 216), it is not absolutely necessary to decide between these various boundaries, it may be well to gain a general knowledge of them, by beginning with extremes, i. e. with the earliest and latest limits of the Ancient period, which have been proposed, and then proceeding to the intermediate lines, or those which have been drawn between them.

§ 220. The earliest limits which have been assigned to the Ancient Period or First Age of Church History are, the beginning of the fourth century (Thiele), when persecution ceased, and the church became united with the state; and the close of the same century, when the empire was finally divided into two, and about to be flooded with barbarians (Koeppen), both which make the First Age too short in proportion to the others for any practical purpose. Nearly coincident with this is Milman's ancient period, to the abolition of paganism in the empire.

§ 221. The latest limit which has been assigned to the same period is the close of the tenth century, the period of the greatest darkness and the most extreme depression; but this is open to an opposite objection.

§ 222. Midway between these two extremes is the close of the seventh century, after the sixth œcumenical council, which seems to have been independently selected as the boundary by several historians of very different schools, such as Alzog (§ 136), Kurtz (§ 135), and Palmer (§ 142), who assigns as a reason, that the equilibrium was now disturbed, the heresies being no longer counterbalanced by the "holy œcumenical councils," nor the losses of the church at home by gains abroad.

§ 223. On either side of this mean line two others have been drawn, which are still more extensively adopted ; first, the end of the sixth century, regarded by many of the older writers as the close of the ancient period and of the series of Church Fathers, and substantially adopted by Neander and his school, because the hierarchy was there complete in the person of the first pope, Gregory the Great. (Guericke, Jacobi, Schaff, Robertson, Hawkins.)

§ 224. Hase, and Kurtz in his earlier works, draw the line at the close of the eighth century, when the centre of gravity was transferred from the Roman to the German side, as represented by Charlemagne and his successors. (Mosheim, Waddington, Lindner, Frick.)

§ 225. Amidst these variations as to precise boundaries, it still remains true that the three great periods are distinct and distinguishable; and while the choice seems to lie between the last two lines, it may be well to retain both, as distinct but compatible divisions, and to look rather at the great characteristic feature, than at the precise bounds of the periods in question.

§ 226. As an aid to the memory, more useful than agreeable to good taste, the three great Periods or Ages may be designated by single words as the periods of Formation, Deformation, and Reformation, or perhaps in better English, as the Forming, Deforming, and Reforming periods, a nomenclature not merely arbitrary, but founded on the mutual relations of the periods, since Reformation implies previous Corruption, and Corruption original formation.

§ 227. But as every period has more than one face or aspect, and cannot therefore be exhaustively described in one word, the three ages may be more precisely though less pointedly distinguished as (I.) the period of Formation and Discipline (not ecclesiastical, but providential); (II.) the period of Consolidation and Corruption (or Petrifaction and Putrefaction), the cessation of activity, however brilliant in appearance (like the reign of Solomon compared with that of David), often coinciding with incipient corruption; (III.) the period of Reformation and Division, the same principle which wrought the one, tending, when pushed to an extreme, to work the other.

§ 228. It would be easy to multiply descriptions of the three great periods or ages, founded upon partial views, and more especially on single aspects of their relative condition, some of which are ingenious and just in theory, though not always practically useful or available.

§ 229. Such is Schaff's description of the first age as that in which the subjective and objective, or the individual and aggregate, constituents of all church history, were held in equilibrio, or kept in due proportion to each other, not so much by a deliberate and conscious effort, as by providential causes; and when these ceased to operate, one of the elements became predominant, and brought to view a new phase of the history.

§ 230. Thus in the Middle Ages, the objective was predominant, the right of private judgment and the sense of personal responsibility being merged in the authority and absolving power of the Church (which is the fatal spell of popery, entirely independent of her ceremonies and external form); while in the third, or present period, the scales are reversed, and the subjective is preponderant, the right of private judgment and the sense of personal responsibility having (among Protestants) almost entirely superseded the authority of the Church.

§ 231. From these vicissitudes already realized, the author ingeniously prognosticates a fourth age, yet to come, in which the equilibrium shall be restored and afterwards maintained, not, as in the first age, by accident or special divine interposition, but by conscious co-operation of the Church itself, enlightened by its previous experience.

§ 232. Entirely different in form and principle, but equally ingenious and one-sided, is the ethnological distinction last proposed by Kurtz, and resting on the theory of three successive forms of civilization, through which the Church is to pass, the Oriental (or Jewish), the Classical or (Greco-Roman), and the Modern (or Germanic in the wide sense of the term including Anglo-Saxon); the first form corresponding to the Old Testament history and the beginning of the Apostolical; the second reaching to the close of the eighth century; and the third belonging to the Modern Ages, the Middle Ages being the transition from the Greco-Roman to the Germanic form of civilization, under which there are included intellectual culture and social condition.

§ 233. As no one of these partial and one-sided views of the difference between the three great periods is sufficient of itself to represent them to the mind, it may be well to combine the truth involved in them with what we know besides as to the character of these three ages, in a general description.

§ 234. The first great feature of the Ancient Period is the rapid simultaneous extension of the Church, and propagation of the gospel, in various directions, but with an impetus decreasing as we draw near to the Middle Ages.

§ 235. Another is the long-continued state of persecution, followed by relief, patronage, establishment or union with the state, and finally enslavement by it and subjection to it.

§ 236. A third characteristic is the gradual expansion and development of church-organization, with an accompanying effort after outward unity, which seems at the close of the first age to be attained, by the consummation of the monarchical development in the primacy of Rome, or the commencement of the papal power, under Gregory the Great.

§ 237. A fourth feature of the Ancient Church is its conflict with error, first in the open and avowed hostility of Judaism and Heathenism, and then in the more covert and insidious enmity of heresies, arising from the mixture of various forms of error with Christianity itself, leading, before the end of this first age, to the discussion and settlement of all the most essential doctrines on their present basis.

§ 238. The last characteristic of the First Age, is the absence of a fixed law or type of Christian experience, there being ample proof that personal religion did exist and flourish, but with a freedom and variety of inner life peculiar to the times, including many eccentricities and aberrations, not without some tokens of incipient corruption.

§ 239. The first great negative distinction of the Middle Age is this, that it originated nothing good, but only evil, while both good and bad things of an older date were still continued, although seldom without some exaggeration or corruption.

§ 240. The unity which seemed to be secured by the erection of the papal see, begins immediately to be dissolved by means of the Great Schism between East and West.

§ 241. The theological or doctrinal distinction of the Middle Age, is the vast expenditure of thought and labor on the mere elaboration of results already gained in new and strange forms, more especially the mystic and scholastic, and the tendency to give these forms a stereotype or petrified rigidity, which, far from lessening or conciliating heresy and error, made them more numerous and desperate than ever.

§ 242. The worst peculiarity of this age is the vast increase of superstition in its various forms, with its invariable accompaniment, moral depravation, both of theory and practice.

§ 243. Its only redeeming or consolatory feature is the under-current of determined opposition to these evils, the reformatory tendency or movement, running through the Middle Ages, never entirely wanting, although varying in strength and clearness, sometimes appearing even in the dominant authorities, at others only among those who were regarded as opponents and directors, if not formally condemned as heretics and schismatics.

§ 244. The first great feature of the Third or Modern Age is the reaction against these great evils, the secession of a large part of the Latin Church, and the assertion of the right of private judgment, with a more or less complete return to apostolical simplicity and purity, all which is summed up in the word Reformation.

§ 245. Another feature not to be neglected, is the influence exerted by this great reaction on the residuary church itself for good and evil, for good in the correction of some errors and abuses, for evil in the aggravation and perpetuation of others.

§ 246. The theology of this age, as distinguished from that of the two others, is learned and critical, with tendencies to scepticism, more or less determined.

§ 247. In addition to the old division of the Greek and Latin Church, and the new division of the latter introduced by the Reformation, this period is characterized by further subdivisions, such as that of the Protestant body into Lutheran and Calvinistic; and of these parts into others, by secession, disruption, or excision.

§ 248. Besides this tendency to subdivision, springing from the use or abuse of the right of private judgment, within the pale of Christianity itself, the third age is distinguished by a rank growth of heresies, both old and new, and by a singular variety of anti-Christian errors, or new forms of infidelity, disowning the authority of Scripture, and abandoning the Christian name.

§ 249. An intermediate division between that of the Centuries and that of the Three Ages, may be obtained by grouping the former, so as at the same time to divide the latter, not by arbitrary lines, but by discriminating things that really differ

§ 250. Thus the Early Age, or Ancient History, may be equally divided, supposing it to consist of six centuries (§ 223), by a line drawn at the close of the third century; the first half differing from the second as a period of persecution from one of establishment; as a period of rapid from one of slower propagation; as a period during which the church was working off heretical admixtures, from one in which it was positively settling the great doctrines of religion.

§ 251. The seventh and eighth centuries may be regarded as a kind of debatable or neutral ground, like a lane, or narrow strip of litigated land between two farms, which may be added to either without materially affecting any thing but its extent.

§ 252. The divisions of the Middle Ages are not so obvious, but a definite basis for them is afforded by the extreme depression of the Church in the 10th century, and by the premonitions of the Reformation in the 14th and 15th.

§ 253. Upon this basis, the Middle Ages may be divided into three unequal parts; the first including centuries VII.—X. (or, according to Hase and Kurtz IX.—.X) during which there was a gradual decline from the position of the ancient Church to its lowest condition in the 10th century; the second including centuries XI.—XIII., during which there was a rise, but in a different direction, a new kind of activity and life, and during which the great peculiar movements of the Age, the Papacy, Scholasticism, Monachism, reached their height and full development; the third including centuries XIV.—XV., during which these same great interests declined, and the reformatory tendency grew proportionally strong and visible. Though the Last or Modern Age comprises only three and a half centuries, each of which has a character or aspect of its own, it may still be divided into two larger portions, each of which has a distinctive character; the first consisting of the 16th and 17th, and characterized by the Reformation and its positive effects, both on the Protestant and Unreformed churches; the other consisting of the 18th and 19th, and characterized by the more negative effects of the same causes. (See below, §§ 273, 274.)

§ 254. Besides all these divisions, it is well to have some characteristic features of each century associated with it in the memory, the points selected being few in number, and, as far as possible, peculiar to the periods with which they are connected.

§ 255. As a mnemonic aid, some use may be made of the Latin nomenclature commonly ascribed to Cave (§ 113), and more or less modified by later writers, viz., 1. Seculum Apostolicum. 2. Gnosticum. 3. Novatianum (v. Cyprianum). 4. Arianum. 5. Nestorianum (Pelagiarum, v. Augustinianum). 6. Entychianum. 7. Monothleticum (v. Muhammedanicum). 8. Iconoclasticum. 9. Photianum (v. Obscurum). 10. Obscurum (v. Tenebrioscum). 11. Hildebrandicum. 12. Waldense. 13. Scholasticum. 14. Wiclifianum. 15. Synodale. 16. Reformatum.

§ 256. In characterizing the first century more particularly, due regard must be had to its unique position, as the period of transition from an old to a new world, from the Jewish to the Christian Church, and from Biblical to Ecclesiastical History, only the smaller part of it belonging strictly to the latter, while the whole may be divided into three nearly equal parts, or into the ministries of John the Baptist and Jesus Christ, of Peter and Paul, and of the Apostle John; with the additional associated names of Nero and Domitian as persecutors, and of Simon Magus and Cerinthus as Heresiarchs.

§ 257. The second century presents the opening of the great twofold conflict of the Church, intellectual and physical, with persecution and brute force on one hand, on the other with Judaism and Heathenism as open enemies, and with heresies arising from their fusion or amalgamation with Christian doctrine; both which conflicts may be associated with the names of Trajan and the Antonines as persecutors; Marcus Aurelius and Celsus as heathen opponents of the truth; Ignatius, Polycarp, and Justin, as martyrs; the latter also representing the Christian Apologists or champions of the truth against its heathen enemies, and the Christian Philosophers, or Platonizing theologians, whose excesses partly caused the Gnostic heresies, of which the great opponent was Tertullian, though himself involved in the very different error of the Montanists.

§ 258. The third century is marked by its disciplinary schisms, represented by Novatian; its catholicism, represented by Cyprian; its Greek or Alexandrian theology and learning represented by Origen, who was also the most eminent opponent of the Monenchian heresies, to which may be added Manicheeism, as a doctrinal feature of the age.

§ 259. The fourth century is marked by the end of persecution under Constantine; the end of paganism under Theodosius; the division of the empire between his sons; the first and second general councils, occasioned by the Arian and Semiarian heresies, of which the chief opponents were Athanasius and the three Cappadocian doctors (Basil and the Gregories), who also favoured and contributed to propagate the new system of ascetic and monastic life.

§ 260. As prominent features of the fifth century may be named the Pelagian, Nestorian, and Eutychian heresies; the third and fourth œcumenical councils, at which they were condemned; Chrysostom, the greatest preacher, Augustin, the greatest theologian; and Jerome, the greatest biblical scholar of the age; the downfall of the western Roman empire; and the conversion of the Franks to Christianity.

§ 261. In the sixth century the series of controversies and of councils is continued by the Monophysite error and the fifth œcumenical council; while additional landmarks are afforded by the legislation and the conquests of Justinian, and by the full development of the hierarchy, in the foundation of the papal power under Gregory the First (or Great).

§ 262. The series of ancient doctrinal controversies closes with that of the Monothelites, and the series of ancient councils with the Sixth and the Quinisextum; but a more important feature of the age is the rise and progress of Mahometanism.

§ 263. This new religion made still further progress in the eight century by the Moorish conquest of Spain, but was repelled from France by Charles Martel, whose son, Charlemagne, revived the Western Empire, and laid the foundation of the temporal power of the Pope by his donations; while the Germans were brought within the pale of the Church chiefly by the labours of Boniface, thence called their Apostle.

§ 264. In the ninth century, the new pretensions of the Papal See were fortified by forged decretals, under the auspices of Nicolas I., who, also, interfered in the eastern strife detween Photius and Ignatius, and thus contributed to the great schism; while the western church was agitated by the predestinarian controversy begun by Godescalcus, and the broaching of the doctrine of transubstantiation by Paschasius Radbert; the reformatory tendency being represented by Claudius of Turin.

§ 265. The 10th century is the lowest depression of the Church at large, and of the papacy in particular, which was a mere slave of political parties; so that we have to look for great names to the world, such as Otho the Great in Germany, and Hugh Capet, the founder of a new dynasty in France; a degradation only partially redeemed by the monastic organization of Clugny, and the nominal conversion of the Scandinavian and Sclavonian races.

§ 266. The 11th century opens with a general panic in relation to the end of the world, followed by a general reaction; and with a partial restoration of the papacy by Gabert or Sylvester II.; followed by some signs of intellectual life in the Berengarian controversy; which is connected, in its turn, with the rise of Hildebrand, afterwards Gregory VII., the founder of the papal theocracy, who carried it out in theory, and in practice as far as he was suffered by the violent resistance of the German Emperors, particularly Henry IV.

§ 267. The 12th century is marked, on one hand, by its chivalry, crusades, and military orders; on the other, by the conflict between mysticism and rationalism, represented by Bernard and Abelard; the first development of scholastic theology, represented by the "Sentences" of Peter Lombard; and a new reformatory movement, represented by Peter Waldo, the reputed founder of the Waldenses;

while the new pretensions of the Papacy were manfully sustained by Alexander III.

§ 268. In the 13th century, all the great medieval interests were carried to their height; the Papal Power by Innocent III.; the Scholastic Theology by Thomas Aquinas; the Monastic Organization by St. Francis and St. Dominic; with the last of whom, or his immediate successors, we may associate the Inquisition.

§ 269. In the 14th century begins the decline of the scholastic theology, with a corresponding rise of mysticism; the end of the Papal Theocracy with Boniface VIII., followed by the Babylonish Captivity and Papal schism; the rise of a vernacular literature in Italy, connected with the great names of Dante and Petrarch; and a powerful attempt at reformation made by Wiclif and the Lollards.

§ 270. In the 15th century, the same work is continued or renewed in Bohemia by John Huss and Jerome of Prague; in France, by the Reforming School of Paris; and in the church at large, by the great Reforming Councils, but without immediate success, although the great end was, more or less, promoted by certain secular events, such as the end of the Greek Empire, the Revival of Letters, the Invention of Printing, and the Discovery of America.

§ 271. The great feature of the 16th century is the Reformation, in its two main branches, German and Swiss, together with its introduction into various countries; whether temporary, as in Spain and Italy; or partial, as in France, Hungary, and Southern Germany; or permanent, as in Northern Germany, Holland, England, Scotland; or exclusive, as in Sweden and Denmark; while in the Unreformed Church, the great features are the Organization of the Jesuits and the Council of Trent.

§ 272. The 17th century is marked by the consolidation of the Protestant churches both in creed and discipline; the religious war of Thirty Years, which ended in the establishment of Protestant rights at the Peace of Westphalia; the Great Rebellion, Commonwealth, and English Revolution, and the introduction of the church into America by colonization.

§ 273. The 18th century may be characterized as a period of revival, revolution, and reaction, the prominent traits of which are Pietism, Moravianism, Methodism, English Deism, French

Philosophy, and German Rationalism; the great Revolutions of America and France.

§ 274. The same features may be traced, through the first half of the 19th century, in the rise and fall of Napoleon; the dismemberment of the Turkish Empire by the Greek Revolution, and of the Spanish Empire by that of Mexico and South America; the second and third French revolutions, and the one now going on in China; the disruption of the Scotch and several American churches; the rise of Unitarianism, Universalism, Irvingism, Puseyism, Socialism, Communism, Mormonism, Spiritualism; while the great redeeming feature of the age is the frequent and extensive revival of religion, and the great benevolent movement in the Protestant churches for the circulation of the Scriptures, and diffusion of religious knowledge, reformation of morals, and eventual conversion of the world, by missionary enterprises, comprehending in their scope Pagans, Mahometans, Jews, and those living under the corrupted forms of Christianity.

§ 275. The centurial and other chronological arrangements, which proceed upon the principle of uniform conventional divisions, have been superseded, in the modern schools of ecclesiastical historiography, by periodologies, or schemes made up of periods, defined, without regard to length or uniformity, by epochs, i. e. turning points or critical junctures, where the current of events, or tide of history, reaches the high-water mark, and the reflux or ebb begins.

§ 276. If the tide or current, to pursue this figure, were a single one, or if the many currents reached their height at once, it would be easy to adopt one general and comprehensive periodology; but as the high tide of one stream or coast is not necessarily or always that of every other, so the crises of history may be variously chosen, and the exercise of this choice by the modern writers, has led to a great diversity of periodologies, or actual arrangements founded on this principle.

§ 277. The exclusive use of any one of these not only makes the others unavailable, but deprives us of the positive advantages attending their comparative or joint use, which are chiefly two; first, increased facility in reading or referring to the words in which they are embodied; and secondly, the aid which they afford in choosing epochs for ourselves, by showing what events have been pointed out as such by eminent historians.

§ 278. In selecting from a multitude of periodologies, devised in modern times, especially in Germany, our choice may be guided by several distinct considerations, such as the celebrity or eminence of the inventor, the extensive use of the arrangement by others, and its intrinsic convenience or utility.

§ 279. When thus selected, they may be arranged for actual comparison, to most advantage, in the order of their dates, as this enables us to trace the gradual process by which they grew out of and improved upon each other.

§ 280. It will be sufficient for our present purpose to confine our view, at least in the first instance, to the periodologies of Gieseler, Neander, Guericke (Jacobi), Hase, Kurtz, and Schaff, as fairly representing the improved modern methods, and affording us the use of what is really most valuable in them all.

§ 281. Among these, Gieseler is entitled to precedence, not only as one of the most eminent, but also as the oldest; for although he speaks of the periodological method as already generally introduced, and of its actual results as already very various, it is easy to perceive from his own arrangement, that the previous attempts were comparatively rude and unsuccessful.

§ 282. In order to illustrate and exemplify the process by which all periodologies are framed, it may be well to give a more particular description of the one proposed by Gieseler, than will be necessary in the case of any other, as the principle and *modus operandi* are substantially the same in all.

§ 283. As a preliminary fact of some importance, it may here be stated, that the modern periodologies vary from each other as to the *terminus a quo* or starting point of Ecclesiastical History; some going back to the Apostolic Age, or to the Life of Christ, and even beyond his birth; while others begin at the close of the New Testament history, e. g. Neander, who has treated the Evangelical and Apostolical History in independent works. On this account, the *terminus a quem* will be considered as a variable line or point, and only stated where it is essential to the completeness or the symmetry of the arrangement.

§ 284. The periodology of Gieseler is determined by the choice of three great turning points or junctures, which he designates as primary epochs :—I. The sole reign of Constantine, without a rival or a colleague, from the year 324. II. The outbreak of the Iconoclastic or Image Controversy in the year 726. III. The Reformation, from Luther's first public acts as a Reformer, in the year 1517.

§ 285. Before and between these primary epochs, Gieseler assumes others, of less prominence, but still distinctly marked, in his opinion, as salient points and critical junctures. These are eight in number, equally distributed among the intervals already marked out by the others.

§ 286. Anterior to the first great epoch, the sole reign of Constantine, the minor or intermediate points are the accession of the Emperor Adrian (A. D. 117), and that of Septimius Severus (193). Between the first and second (the Iconoclastic controversy), he assumes, as secondary epochs, the Council of Chalcedon (451), and the Monothelite controversy, with the contemporaneous rise of the Mahometan religion (622). Between the second and third (the Reformation), his subsidiary epochs are the Pontificate of Nicolas I., and the Pseudodecretals forged with his connivance (858), and the transfer of the Papal See from Rome to Avignon (1035). Between his third grand epoch and his own time, he assumes, as intermediate points, the

Peace of Westphalia (1648), and the fall of Napoleon (1814).

§ 287. By the major and minor epochs thus assumed, the whole field is divided into four great periods, and each of these subdivided into three others, making twelve in all

§ 288. Gieseler's first great period extends from the beginning of the subject to the sole reign of Constantine (324); his second to the outbreak of the Image controversy (726); his third to the Reformation (1517); his fourth to the date of his last volume (1848).

§ 289. The first subdivision of his first great period ends with Adrian (117); the second with Septimius Severus (193); the third with Constantine (324).

§ 290. The first subdivision of his second great period ends with the Council of Chalcedon (451); the second with Mahomet (622); the third with the Iconoclasts (726).

§ 291. The first subdivision of his third great period ends with Nicolas I. (858); the second with the transfer of the Papal See to Avignon (1305); the third with the Reformation (1517).

§ 292. The first subdivision of his fourth great period ends with the peace of Westphalia (1648); the second with the fall of Napoleon (1814); the third with his own times (1848).

§ 293. These subdivisions may be also arranged in a continued series, with some advantage to the eye and memory. 1. To Adrian (117). 2. To Septimius Severus (193). 3. To Constantine (324). 4. To the Council of Chalcedon (451). 5. To Mahomet (622). 6. To the Iconoclasts (726). 7. To Nicolas I. (858). 8. To the transfer of the Papal See (1305). 9. To the Reformation (1517). 10. To the Peace of Westphalia (1648). 11. To the fall of Napoleon (1814). 12. To our own times (1848).

§ 294. This periodology bears upon its face sufficient indications of its being an early, although not a first, attempt at such arrangements; so that it has met with little currency among later writers, either as a whole, or with respect to some of its particular distinctions and divisions.

§ 295. Specific faults, which have been charged upon it, are the excessive number of its subdivisions, and the arbitrary character of some of his distinctions; for example, the selection of the Image Controversy as one of his great epochs, although less important in its general historical relations than some others which might have been selected; and the same objection has been made to several of his subdivisions, for example, to the first, second, fourth, seventh, eighth. (§ 293.)

§ 296. Few if any of these criticisms can be made upon Neander's Periodology, which greatly excels Gieseler's in simplicity and symmetry, as well as in the choice of the particular divisions; whether this superiority arises from his having designedly improved upon his predecessor, or, which is made more probable by the remarkable diversity between them, from an independent exercise of taste and judgment.

§ 297. Instead of Gieseler's four great periods and twelve subdivisions, Neander assumes six great periods, without any (chronological) subdivisions. His first period reaches to the end of the Diocletian Persecution, on the accession of Constantine the Great (A. D. 312); the second to the pontificate of Gregory the Great (590); the third to the death of Charlemagne (814); the fourth to Hildebrand or Gregory VII. (1073); the fifth to Boniface VIII. (1294); the sixth to Luther or the Reformation (1517).

§ 298. Guericke, one of Neander's most faithful followers (§ 131), adopts his periods, completes them by adding, as a seventh, from the Reformation to the date of his own last edition (1846), and groups the seven in three Ages, the first instance known to me of this arrangement. (§§ 213, 214).

§ 299. Guericke's division into Ages is unequal and irregular, assigning two of Neander's periods to the first Age, four to the second, and making the third co-extensive with the seventh period, added by himself.

§ 300. The same division into Ages is adopted by Neander's other follower and condenser, Jacobi, and the same subdivision of the first or Early Age, beyond which his published work has not yet gone. (§ 132.)

§ 301. The next periodology, in point of time, is that of Hase, originally published a year after Guericke's, agreeing with it in the general distribution, but exhibiting a great improvement on it in simplicity and symmetry, as might have been expected from the tastes and habits of the author, who appears to care at least as much for manner as for matter, for the form as for the substance, of Church History. (§ 133.)

§ 302. Hase, like Guericke, divides the whole into Ancient, Medieval, and Modern Church History, but takes as the dividing line between the first and second, not the end of the sixth century, or the pontificate of Gregory the Great (590), but the institution of the German or new Western Empire by the coronation of Charlemagne (800). (See § 224.)

§ 303. Each of his ages or great periods is divided into two by a single intermediate epoch; the first by Constantine (312); the second by Innocent III. (1216); the third by the Peace of Westphalia (1648).

§ 304. This periodology of Hase is adopted, with a slight modification, by another popular historian, Kurtz (§ 135), who, in his earlier and smaller works, down to the last edition (1856), divides into the same three Ages, but as a line of subdivision in the second, for the death of Innocent III. (1216), substitutes the accession of Boniface VIII. (1294), an epoch belonging to the same century, but marking another stage in the progress of the papacy, and probably adopted for the sake of a closer assimilation to Neander's method. (§ 297.)

§ 305. In Kurtz's larger work, which is not yet

finished, he adopts a different arrangement, founded on the theory of three civilizations (§ 232), according to which the work, so far as it has yet been published, and so far as it relates to Ecclesiastical History in the strict sense (§ 32), is divided into two great Phases, so called, and not Periods or Ages, because not entirely successive but to some extent collateral or parallel, and therefore properly described as Phases, or partly contemporary aspects of the same objective matter.

§ 306. The first Phase, according to this scheme, is the developement of Christianity under the ancient classic form of civilization, from the end of the Apostolic Age to the downfall of the Eastern or Greek Empire (1453). The second Phase is its developement under the medieval or Germanic form of civilization, from the fourth to the fifteeth century inclusive.

§ 307. Each of these Phases is chronologically subdivided by two minor or intermediate lines; the first by the end of the Diocletian persecution (312), and by that of the series of ancient councils (692); the second by the close of the ninth and twelfth centuries respectively.

§ 308. The most finished of these modern periodologies, because combining the advantages and shunning the defects of those which preceded it, is that of Schaff, in which the general arrangement is the same with that of Kurtz and Hase, and the subdivision no less symmetrical in form, while in fulness of detail it is neither so minute as Gieseler nor so meagre as Hase.

§ 309. Schaff divides the whole into three Ages: I. The Primitive or Græco-Latin Church, from Pentecost to Gregory the Great (590). II. The Medieval Church, or Romano-Germanic Catholicism, from Gregory the Great to Luther (1517). III. The Modern or Evangelical Protestant Church, in conflict with the Church of Rome, from Luther to our own time (1853).

§ 310. Each of these Ages he divides into three periods; the first into the period of the Apostolical church until the death of John (100); that of the Persecuted Church to Constantine (311); and that of the Established Church of the Græco-Roman Empire, to Gregory the Great (590).

§ 311. The second he divides into the Rise of the Middle Age, or the planting of the church among the Germanic races, till the appearance of Hildebrand (1049); the Height of the Middle Age

(Papacy, Monachism, Scholasticism, Mysticism), to Boniface VIII. (1303); and the decline of the Middle Age, and preparation for approaching changes, until Luther (1517).

§ 312. The third he divides into the period of the Reformation, or Productive Protestantism and Reacting Romanism (century XVI.); that of Orthodox-confessional and scholastic Protestantism, in conflict with ultramontane Jesuitism and semi-Protestant Jansenism (to the middle of century XVIII.); and that of negative subjective Protestantism—Rationalism and Sectarianism—with premonitions of a new or fourth age (to the middle of the 19th century).

§ 313. These smaller periods, like those of Gieseler (§ 293), may be also arranged in a continued series: 1. To the death of John (100). 2. To Constantine (311). 3. To Gregory the Great (590). 4. To Hildebrand (1049). 5. To Boniface VIII. (1294). 6. To Luther (1517). 7. To the end of the 16th century. 8. To the middle of the 18th. 9. To the middle of the 19th.

§ 314. With these select periodologies, when thoroughly mastered and familiar, it may be improving to compare some others, in a more rapid, and less thorough manner, for the purpose of observing both their general agreement, and the points, whether great or small, in which they differ.

§ 315. Engelhardt assumes five great epochs, I. The conversion of Constantine, and consequent establishment of Christianity in the Roman Empire. II. The rise of Mahometanism, and consequent contraction of the Church, particularly in the East. III. The reaction of the West against this hostile power in the Crusades, and the elevation of the hierarchy to a monarchy. IV. The Reformation, as the beginning of a new age and a thorough change throughout the Church. V. The securing of the civil rights of Protestants, in the Peace of Westphalia as a condition of their free developement.

§ 316. With these epochs he defines six periods: 1. From Christ to Constantine (625). 2. From Constantine to Mahomet (600). 3. From Mahomet to Gregory VII. (1073). 4. From Gregory to Luther (1517). 5. From the Reformation to the Peace of Westphalia (1648). 6. From the Peace of Westphalia to his own time (1830).

§ 317. The simplest periodology is that of Thiele, who assumes the three divisions which are common to almost all arrangements: I. From Christ to Constantine. II. From Constantine to Luther. III. From Luther to his own time (1840).

§ 318. Lobegott Lange has five periods, corresponding to as many stages in the progress of the hierarchy. The first extends to the Council of Nice (325); the second to the developement of the Romish monocratical hierarchy, under Gregory the Great (590); the third to its completion under Gregory the Seventh (in the last third of the eleventh century); the fourth to its decline and fall in many states of Europe at the Reformation (in the first third of the sixteenth century); the fifth from the Reformation to his own time (1846).

§ 319. Two of these periods are subdivided: the first into (1) the period of Primitive Christianity (Urchristenthum) until the developement of Ecclesiastical Hierarchy, and (2) the interval between that and the developement of the Aristocratical Hierarchy; the fourth into the (1) Decline and (2) Fall of the Romish Monocratic Hierarchy.

§ 320. Niedner, one of the most profound and accurate modern German Church Historians, but, at the same time, one of the most obscure and intricate, adopts the division into three great periods or

Ages, but terminates the first in the middle of the eighth century, and the second at the end of the 15th; subdividing the three ages very unequally, the first, besides the Apostolical and earlier history, into (1) the conflict with Græco-Roman heathenism (second and third centuries), (2) with oriental heathenism (fourth, fifth, and sixth centuries); (3) with Islam and Heathendom in the East and West (seventh and eighth centuries); the Second or Middle Age into the Foundation of the Medieval Church (from the middle of the eighth to the middle of the 11th century), its completion (from the middle of the 11th to the end of the 13th), and its decline (during the 14th and 15th); the Third or Modern Age into (1) the Reformation, or the conflict of Protestantism and Roman Catholicism (during the 16th century); (2) the Ecclesiastical and Doctrinal developement of both (to the middle of the 18th century); (3) the scientific and sceptical developement of Protestantism (to the middle of the 19th century).

§ 321. Lindner, a younger writer of great merit, assumes three Ages, the first being that of the developement of Christianity in the Græco-Roman form (during the first eight centuries); the second the strife of the Græco-Roman and Germanic civilization (during the next seven centuries); the third the triumph of Germanic culture in the Reformation (during the last three centuries).

§ 322. He divides each age into two smaller periods, and characterizes each of these, first "politically," then "dogmatically;" his first period, extending to 311, being that of the church under heathen persecution, and employed in excluding the Judaic and heathen element from its theology; the second, extending to 814, that of its establishment and ultimate subjection to the state.

§ 323. In the Middle Ages, his first period, extending to 1294, is that of the subjection of the state to the church, and of the civil to the canon law, and also that of the scholastic reproduction of theology, together with the first signs of reaction and reformatory movement; his second period, extending to 1517, is that of the emancipation of the state from the thraldom of the hierarchy, and the developement of nationalities, and also that of conflict between the Roman and Germanic mind in doctrinal discussion, with still clearer marks of a reforming tendency.

§ 324. In the third Age, Lindner's first division, extending to 1648, is the period of Protestant triumph over Popish oppression, but subjection to the Protestant state, and of purified doctrine in conflict with Roman stiffness and enthusiastic laxity; his second period is that of pietistical reaction against church and state, and effort after free organization, together with the conflict of the true doctrine with the extreme forms of pietism and rationalism.

§ 325. Fricke retains the usual distinction of three Ages, but terminates the first at Charlemagne's original accession to the throne (768), and describes it as comprising the rise of Christianity till the settlement of the great doctrines and of the constitution in the form of papal monarchy; the second as the period or age of doctrinal stagnation and of papal usurpation, with opposition and reaction, both in church and state; the third as the age of advancing freedom and political security, popish reaction and revival, Protestant orthodox rigidity, and general effort after peace and union not yet realized.

§ 326. The German Roman Catholic Church historian Abzog (§ 136) also adopts the favourite division into three Ages and six periods, the first age being that of the Church in the Græco-Roman Empire, and comprising the first seven centuries; the second that of the Church in the Germanic and Slavonic races, from the fourth to the 15th century, inclusive; the third from the "Western Schism," as he calls the Reformation, to the present time. The first age he divides, as usual, by Constantine (313); the second he divides by the accession of Gregory VII. (1073), and subdivides by the death of Charlemagne (814), and Boniface VIII. (1303); the third age he divides by the Peace of Westphalia (1648).

§ 327. Very different from this, and evidently calculated for the meridian of France not Germany, is the periodology of the ultramontane French historian Postel (§ 136), who assumes eleven periods, 1. From Christ to Constantine (313). 2. To the fall of the Western Empire (476). 3. To Mahomet (622.) 4. To the death of Charlemagne (814). 5. To the first crusade (1095). 6. To the death of St. Louis (1270). 7. To the fall of the Eastern Empire (1453). 8. To the close of the Council of Trent (1563), including the Reformation (§ 217). 9. To the death of Louis XIV. (1715). 10. To the elevation of Pius VII. (1800). 11. To the elevation of Pius IX. (1846).

§ 328. Of the recent English writers on Church History (§ 141), Hardwick treats only of the Middle Ages and the Reformation; Blunt of the first three centuries; Robertson of the first six, which he divides like Neander, whose periods are also adopted by Waddington. (§ 140.)

§ 329. Somewhat different is the periodology of Palmer (§ 142), though he likewise assumes five great periods without subdivision: I. That of the Pure and Persecuted Church (to 320). II. That of Heresies and Holy Œcumenical Councils (to 680). III. That of Ignorance, Worldliness, and Superstition, with pious reaction and extensive conversions (to 1054). IV. That of Schism between the East and West, and of the height and decline of the Papal usurpation (to 1517). V. That of Reformation and Resistance, Schism and Infidelity (to 1839).

§ 330. The periodology of Milman (§ 139), is confused by extreme minuteness and by complication with a topical arrangement, so that it is not easily compared with those already mentioned, but deserves attention, not only on account of his general celebrity, but as a key to his two important works upon Church History.

§ 331. Milman's first work (§ 139) extends from the birth of Christ to the abolition of Paganism in the Roman Empire, and is divided into books and chapters, partly on a chronical and partly on a topical method. His second work, the History of Latin Christianity, extends to the Pontificate of Nicolas V. and is divided by the author into fourteen Periods, as he calls them, although some of them are not strictly Periods but Topics.

§ 332. The first of these "Periods" extends to the Pontificate of Damasus and his two successors (366–401); the second to Leo the Great (461); the third to the death of Gregory the Great (604); the fourth to the coronation of Charlemagne (800); the fifth to the end of his dynasty (996); the sixth includes the series of German Pontiffs (1061); the seventh that of Italian Pontiffs, beginning with Gregory VII. (1073); the eighth the strife about investiture (during the 12th century); the ninth the height of the Papacy, to the formation of the Canon Law, under Gregory IX. (1238); the tenth the conflict of the Popes and Emperors (to the death of Innocent IV. 1254); the eleventh the triumph of the Papacy until broken under Boniface VIII. (who died 1303); the twelfth the Babylonian Captivity till 1370; the thirteenth the Papal schism, the reforming councils, and attempts at union with the Greeks; the fourteenth medieval art and revival of letters. A concluding topic is the advance of reformation and the rivalry of Latin and Teutonic Christianity.

§ 333. From the definition previously given (§ 275) of the periodological arrangement, it will be seen that it makes use of epochs only to define its periods, as the surveyor plants his stakes for the purpose of his measurements or observations, and when these are finished, removes or leaves them, which he would not if the stakes had an intrinsic value, or were useful for another purpose.

§ 334. Now the epochs used in framing periodologies are also valuable in themselves, or independently of this use, as salient and turning points in history, to know which is a wide step towards the knowledge of the history itself, but to select which the beginner is incompetent, unless assisted by the judgment of the best historians, as expressed in the selection of particular epochs as the basis or the framework of their periodologies.

§ 335. In order to apply them to this use, it will be found a salutary exercise to separate them from the periodologies of which they form a part, especially when this is done, not by mere transcription or dictation, but by the personal exertions of the individual student, to encourage which the following suggestions are presented, drawn from personal experience.

12

§ 336. Let all the epochs be collected from as many distinct periodologies as may be thought desirable, for instance from the twenty which have been described in the preceding paragraphs (§§ 284–332) or from the six selected specimens first stated, and placed in a continued series, without reference to their position in the several periodological arrangements.

§ 337. Then let this aggregate or gross amount be reduced by eliminating all that does not properly fall under the description of an epoch, as for instance when a century, or half a century, its first third, or its last third, are employed as periodological distinctions, these being not real epochs, but expedients borrowed from the old centurial method.

§ 338. Let the list thus shortened be reduced still further by consolidating dates which really represent one epoch—such as the six dates in the reign of Constantine, his accession (311), his decrees of toleration (312, 313), the beginning of his sole reign (323, 324), and the first Œcumenical Council (325); or the two dates in the life of Gregory the Great, his accession (590) and his death (604); or the corresponding points in the history of Boniface VIII. (1294 and 1303); or the three in that of Charlemagne, his original accession (768), his coronation as Emperor (800), and his death (814); or the two in that of Gregory VII., his original appearance (1049), and his election to the Papacy (1073); or the two dates assigned to the beginning of the Reformation (the beginning of the century and the year 1517).

§ 339. The epochs thus reduced in number, may be then distributed by centuries, not as a permanent arrangement, but for the purpose of observing the difference between the centuries, as to the frequency or paucity of critical or turning points, some having none in the preceding periodologies (viz. the 1st, 3d, and 12th), some only one (viz. the 6th, 10th, and 17th), some two (viz. the 2d, 9th, 15th, 16th, and 18th), some three (viz. the 8th and 14th), some four (viz. the 5th, 7th, and 19th), some five (viz. the 11th and 13th), and one seven (viz. the 4th, if every date be separately counted), but if all that really belong together be consolidated, only two. These differences, although to some extent fortuitous, must have some basis in the true relations of the several centuries to one another.

§ 340. Another method of comparison is to observe how many of the given periodologies agree in recognizing any epoch, which may be regarded as an indication of the extent to which it is acknowledged by historians as a turning point or critical juncture.

§ 341. By the application of this process to the periodologies which have been described, it will be found that the Reformation has a place in twelve, the reign of Constantine in ten, that of Charlemagne in nine, the pontificate of Boniface VIII. in eight, that of Gregory VII. in seven, that of Gregory the Great in six, and the Peace of Westphalia in an equal number.

§ 342. Next to the epochs which are thus found in from half a dozen to a dozen modern periodologies, and may therefore be regarded as the most extensively acknowledged, we may place a second class, containing such as have a place in three periodologies, as the third French Revolution, or in two, as the appearance of Mahomet in the seventh century, the close of the series of great councils near the end of the same, and the fall of the Greek Empire in the middle of the fifteenth.

§ 343. To these two classes may be added a residuary class of indefinite extent, containing all those epochs which are found in only one periodology, and which are therefore recommended only by the voice of individual historians, but which may nevertheless be real junctures in the history, and therefore valuable aids in understanding and retaining it.

§ 344. From the periodologies described above, omitting some dates which seem to be ill-chosen and unsuited to the end proposed, especially in Milman's list (§ 332), we may obtain the following residuary catalogue, arranged in chronological order. The reign of Adrian (117), Septimius Severus (193), Pontificate of Damasus (366), Council of Chalcedon (451), Leo the Great (461), Fall of the Western Empire (476), Iconoclasm (726), Nicolas I. (858), End of Carlovingian Dynasty (996), Breach between East and West (1054), First Crusade (1095), Death of Innocent III. (1216), Gregory IX. and the Canon Law (1238), Death of St. Louis (1270), Babylonish Captivity (1305), Papal Schism (1375), End of Tridentine Council (1563), Death of Louis XIV. (1715), Accession of Pius VII. (1800), Fall of Napoleon (1814), Second French Revolution (1830), Accession of Pius IX. (1846).

§ 345. The best mode of using the epochs thus arranged and classed, is first to master those of the first order, as most generally recognized; and then, when these are perfectly familiar, to pursue the same course with the second, after which the residuary class can be gradually added, and at the same time indefinitely enlarged.

§ 346. Another useful method of the same kind is to frame successively lists or tables, each containing nineteen dates, or one for every century, the choice of which, if made by the student himself, involves an exercise of mind which must be useful in proportion to the difficulties that attend it.

§ 347. The following may be taken as a specimen of such a table, not to be permanently rested in, but often and indefinitely varied. Century I. the fall of Jerusalem (70), II. Martyrdom of Justin (163), III. Decian Persecution (250), IV. Council of Nice (325), V. Fall of Western Empire (476), VI. Gregory the Great (590), VII. Mahomet (622), VIII. Iconoclasm (726), IX. Death of Charlemagne (814), X. Accession of Otho the Great (936), XI. Gregory VII. (1073), XII. Alexander III. (1159), XIII. Boniface VIII. (1294), XIV. Wiclif (1360), XV. Fall of Eastern Empire (1453), XVI. Luther (1517), XVII. Peace of Westphalia (1648), XVIII. Wesley (1732), XIX. Fall of Napoleon (1814).

§ 348. When the points in such a list are really salient, they will indicate, in some degree, the great changes as they follow one another; as for instance in the table just presented, although not framed with any such design, we find martyrdom (century II.) and persecution (III.) followed by the first Œcumenical Council (IV.); the degradation of the Church in the ninth and 10th centuries suggested by the choice of emperors to represent them; the subsequent rise of the papacy by the choice of three popes to represent as many centuries (XI. XII. XIII.), its decline and the growth of the reformatory tendency, by the position here assigned to Wiclif (XIV.), &c., &c.

§ 349. Such tables may be constructed either on the principle of varying the epochs, i. e. choosing sometimes one kind of event and then another; or on that of sameness, making all the points in any given table similar to one another, e. g. making out a series of great councils or assemblies, beginning with the Council at Jerusalem in the first century, and ending with the First Free Church Assembly in the nineteenth; or, finally, avoiding both extremes, as in the specimen first given.

§ 350. The materials for such lists may be drawn, in the first instance, from the periodologies already given; then from the topical details to be given hereafter; thirdly, from books of history, whether thoroughly studied or skimmed over for this very purpose; and lastly from the chronological tables, found in most such books or elsewhere, which last, however, unless used with moderation, will deprive the student of the benefit arising from his own exertions.

§ 351. Having taken our first or chronological survey of the whole field, we may now proceed, in execution of our plan (§ 207), to the second or topical survey of the same ground, beginning, as before, with the definition of terms, suggested by their etymology.

§ 352. From the Greek τόπος meaning *place*, comes (1) the adjective *topical*, used in medicine as the equivalent of *local*, from the Latin *locus*, and (2) the noun topic, applied by the ancient writers in a peculiar technical sense to certain parts of rhetoric and logic, as in the *topics* of Aristotle and Cicero, and in theology to the usual divisions (*loci communes*) of the system of doctrine (whence our popular usage of *commonplace* for that which is familiar, trite, or hackneyed), but in history and other sciences to their subdivisions or constituent parts.

§ 353. The name is not properly applied to insulated facts, as such considered, which are rather *anecdotes*, in the technical sense of the term, as denoting, primarily, inedited, unpublished facts, and then detached or separate historical materials; the accessory idea of something humorous or entertaining being altogether popular and adventitious.

§ 354. The same fact or event which, in itself considered, is an *anecdote*, as just defined, may be a *topic* when regarded as holding a specific place in history considered as a systematic whole.

§ 355. But although the meaning of the word has been determined, a question still presents itself, in reference to the thing which it denotes. What constitutes a topic? and how are the topics of Church History in particular to be determined?

§ 356. Not every individual fact—nor even every great event—can be regarded as constituting a distinct historical topic; because such fact or event may be inseparable from others, or at least from its own minor and accompanying circumstances; just as in a landscape, a particular object, as a tree or house, may be so situated with respect to others, that it cannot be surveyed apart, or constitute a separate object of vision. This is sometimes true of a whole series of successive events or a whole congeries of contemporary facts, which must be viewed together, in order to constitute a definite historical topic.

§ 357. We may now complete the definition of a topic, so far as it is necessary for our purpose, as a fact, or a series or a group of facts, forming one definite object of historical investigation, and occupying a definite place in history, considered as a systematic whole.

§ 358. The essential element in this complex idea, that of distinct objectivity, may vary in the case of different persons, some being able or accustomed to take in more at a single view than others; so that no selection or arrangement of topics is to be regarded as alone admissible exclusively of every other.

§ 359. Even in one and the same topical arrangement, it is best not to aim at an exact uniformity, either in quantity or quality, but to let it be controlled by circumstances, the topic being sometimes one event, such as the death of Julius Cæsar, and at other times a series or system of events, such as the Reformation or the French Revolution.

§ 360. This liberty of choice, and flexibility of method, far from being a defect or disadvantage, as compared with mathematical rigour and exactness, is one of the great charms of historical study, and its loss one of the worst effects of all exclusive methods.

§ 361. There are two methods of selecting and arranging historical topics, which may be distinguished as the Analytic and Synthetic, in the strict etymological sense and application of those terms.

§ 362. The synthetic method begins with the minute details, and groups them, first in smaller, then in larger combinations, so as finally to form great masses; while the analytic method takes these masses, and divides and subdivides, eliminates and simplifies, until it reaches the constituent elements with which the synthesis began.

§ 363. While both these processes are useful in their proper place, and may be both employed alternately, though not together, the last is better suited to our purpose, since by descending from generals to particulars, a basis is secured for the future study of details; whereas minute attention to the latter could extend to but a few, even of these, without imparting any general views whatever.

§ 364. For the study of a lifetime, or for original investigations, similar to those of Gieseler or Neander, the synthetic method may be best, but not for a brief academical course, wholly preparatory in its purpose.

§ 365. Another distinction which may possibly be useful is, that between two ways of viewing the particular topics when determined or selected; either, on the one hand, as mere subdivisions of an organic whole, without individual vitality or separate existence, like the counties in a State, or the departments in France; or, on the other hand, as so many organic wholes, forming a greater whole by federal combination, like the Swiss cantons or the States of our Union.

§ 366. Though both these views involve some truth, and may be turned to good account, the first is better suited to the exact sciences than to history, which consists in the aggregation of innumerable facts, not necessarily dependent on each other, and yet all related, and susceptible of rational as well as arbitrary combination.

§ 367. Instead, therefore, of assuming certain periods, and then cutting these into strips or slices by a uniform or rubrical division, we may let each topic reach as far as it will, or as we find convenient, using chronological divisions, not to cut them up, but simply to mark the surface, like the shadow on a dial.

§ 368. Ecclesiastical History, thus viewed, is a

congeries of minor histories, each of which is, in a certain sense, complete within itself, but in another sense, incomplete without the rest.

§ 369. The number, size, and form of these minor histories is not determined by the nature of the subject, or by any other extrinsic necessity, but is variable and discretionary, so that no exclusive method is either practicable or desirable.

§ 370. So great is this variety and liberty of combination, that the same event may enter into more than one of these particular histories, or may be treated both as a separate topic and as a component of one more extensive.

§ 371. It would be easy to divide the whole field of Ecclesiastical History into a few great topics or minor histories, running through its entire chronological dimensions; such as the history of Missions or of Church Extension, that of Church Organization, that of Doctrine, &c. But this would be only a slight modification of the rubrical method, on a larger scale, and therefore more unmanageable than when divided into centuries or periods.

§ 372. The same objection does not lie against some other similar divisions, such as the biographical division into lives, or personal histories, or that into the history of Councils, Controversies, Churches; all which have their own advantages, but none of which can possibly be made to comprehend all the materials or topics of Church History.

§ 373. The best method therefore is, instead of any uniform and rigid rule of distribution and arrangement, to select the topics for ourselves, taking sometimes one event and sometimes many, as the subject of investigation, and dividing and combining them to suit our own convenience, and the end which we have immediately in view.

§ 374. The general arrangement must of course be chronological; because all history, from its very nature, is so; because this order throws the most light on the mutual relation of events; and because it gives the most aid to the student's memory.

§ 375. In selecting the topics of Ecclesiastical History, it is best to begin with some connecting link between it and Biblical History—some event whose causes reach back and their effects forward, so as to touch both great divisions of the subject.

§ 376. Such an event is the destruction of Jerusalem, A. D. 70, only six or seven years after the close of the New Testament history, and yet many years before the probable date of the Apocalypse.

§ 377. But besides its date, it is also recommended by the connection of its causes and effects with the history of the Church.

§ 378. The proximate causes of this great catastrophe were the growing fanaticism and insubordination of the zealots, on one hand, and the cowardly but cruel domination of the Roman procurators on the other; both which causes seem to have grown worse and worse after the death of Christ, as if in execution of a special divine judgment.

§ 379. Our principal authority in reference to this great event is Flavius Josephus, a Jew of sacerdotal lineage, and a commander in the Jewish war, but afterwards highly favoured by the Romans, and therefore accused by his own people of apostasy, and regarded by many Christians also as unworthy of belief, while others go to the opposite extreme of preferring his testimony to that of the Scriptures; the truth, as usual in such cases, lying between the two.

§ 380. The providential instruments of this destruction were the Roman armies, first under Vespasian, and when he was recalled to Rome by the death of Vitellius, under his son Titus, the deliciæ humani generis, who used to say "Perdidi diem " when he had performed no act of beneficence; a character probably exaggerated by the heathen writers, and measured by the heathen standard, but the comparative excellence of which is proved by his conduct in this siege, when Jews and Gentiles seemed to have changed places, the impious desperation of the former being strangely contrasted with the moderation and humanity of Titus.

§ 381. The details of this event may be found in Josephus, Prideaux, Milman, Kurtz, and others; we are concerned only with its religious and ecclesiastical effects.

§ 382. Its effects upon the Jews has reference to their government, their religion, and their persecutions.

§ 383. The political effect was to destroy the Hebrew state or commonwealth, virtually at once, finally and formally, under Adrian, when an insurrection, under a false Messiah, called Barlochba, led to the demolition of the city, the erection of another under the name of Capitolina, and the expulsion of the Jews from Palestine, since which time they have had no existence as a nation or a body politic.

§ 384. As the Hebrew Church was a theocracy,

in which church and state were not only united but identified, the Jewish religion, as distinguished from the Christian, fell with the state, having no local sanctuary, and the ceremonial service being almost entirely abandoned; Providence thus stamping Jewish unbelief as not only wicked but absurd, by making the continuance of the temporary system practically impossible.

§ 385. It was not an exchange of ceremonial for spiritual worship, since this existed before, and the Jews themselves admit the continued obligation of the former, and expect its restoration under the Messiah.

§ 386. A third effect upon the Jews was the cessation of their persecutions, the spirit of which however was perpetuated in their schools and controversies, with a rancour which has been abundantly repaid by Christians.

§ 387. The primary effect of the destruction of Jerusalem on the Christian Church was to put an end to the Judaic controversy, by rendering the observance of the Jewish law impossible.

§ 388. Some Jewish Christians still adhered to it, with more or less tenacity, and thus gave rise to

Jewish-Christian sects, the first of which we have any information.

§ 389. These were distinguished from the body of Christians by their observance of the law, and from the Jews by owning the Messiahship of Jesus.

§ 390. They differed among themselves as to the necessity of the law, the person of Christ, and the authority of Paul.

§ 391. Some denied the absolute necessity of the law; some affirmed it only of Jewish converts; while others made it absolute and universal.

§ 392. Some regarded Christ as a mere man, others as something more, preternaturally born, and endowed with extraordinary gifts; others as a divine person.

§ 393. Some rejected Paul as an apostate, others owned him as an apostle.

§ 394. Our information as to these Jewish Christians is derrived from Justin Martyr, Irenæus, Tertullian, Origen, Epiphanius, and Jerome; but it is very fragmentary and obscure.

§ 395. It is common to assume two sects, differing in the intensity of their Judaic prejudices, the Nasareans and Ebionites.

§ 396. The Nasareans or Nazarenes, a name originally given to all followers of Christ (Acts 24, 6), were the less Jewish class, who held the lowest views as to the law, and the highest as to Christ and Paul.

§ 397. The name of Ebionite is derived by Tertullian from a man named Ebion, a very common ancient practice when the real derivation was unknown; but by Origen more correctly from the Hebrew אֶבְיוֹן poor; whether assumed by themselves as being "poor in spirit," or the Lord's Poor (like the Pauperes of the Middle Ages); or given in contempt by others, as belonging to the lower orders, or perhaps with reference to the poverty of the Mother Church, which some ascribe to the community of goods.

§ 398. The Ebionites were the more Jewish class, who held the lowest views of Christ and Paul, and insisted on the observance of the law as necessary to salvation.

§ 399. When they arose is not positively known, perhaps immediately after the destruction of Jerusalem—they were still in existence in the second century—perhaps much longer, and perhaps were merged in other sects (e. g. the Elcesaites).

§ 400. The gospel of the Nasareans and Ebionites is mentioned by the Fathers, but whether as a creed or as a book is uncertain. Some identify it with the Gospel of the Hebrews, and others with the original of Matthew; which leads us to another topic.

§ 401. Second connecting link—Definition of Ecclesiastical History (§§ 32, 33).—Terminus a quo—close of history in Canon. Hence the question—When was the Canon closed? Details belong to Introduction—or to New Testament History—but outlines to beginning of Ecclesiastical History.

§ 402. Objective close of Canon—when last book written—reign of Domitian—near the end of the first century.—Subjective close of the Canon—when the question was finally determined in and by the Church.

§ 403. Eusebian classification—A. Homologumena—4 Gospels—Acts—13 Epistles of Paul—1 of Peter—1 of John. B. Antilegomena—(*a*) Hebrews (but only as to authors). (*b*) Apocalypse—first owned—then disowned by rationalists and anti-chiliasts—then re-owned. (*c*) James (considered by some antipauline)—2d Peter—2d and 3d John—Jude—all short, and little quotable matter. C. Notha—wholly apocryphal and spurious.

§ 404. Doubts gradually cleared up—Church

became unanimous—not by authority of councils—these as yet only local—and mere witnesses—not judges—special Council of Laodicea (A. D. 360)—and Council of Hippo (393)—our present Canon, established by the 3d Council at Carthage (397).

§ 405. Not a mere passive acquiescence—or random choice—modern German fallacy—criticism unknown to the ancient Church—one of its most important functions—to separate the Canon from the mass of competitors—the *νόθα* of Eusebius (§ 403).

§ 406. These of early origin—even Luke alludes to previous unauthorized attempts to write the Life of Christ—though not necessarily false—yet such would naturally spring up with the true. But

§ 407. Apocryphal literature flourished chiefly in the second century—much of it now lost—but enough left to show its character and origin—which was chiefly heretical—a rank growth from the soil of error—sp. Jewish-Christian sects and gnostics—Epiphanius speaks of "thousands" of gnostic apocrypha—Irenæus (more judicious, moderate, and ancient) of an "inenarrabilis multitudo apocryphorum et perperûm Scripturarum," among the Valentinians alone.

§ 408. Some not heretical—only pious frauds—

vaticinia post eventum—or intended to fill chasms in Canonical books—now impossible—but then facilitated by unsettled Canon.

§ 409. Some claimed a place in Old Testament—some in New Testament Canon—Apocryphal Gospels—Acts—Epistles—Apocalypses—Principal collective editors—Fabricius—Thilo—Tischendorf.

§ 410. Classification of Apocryphal Gospels—I. Those claiming to be complete histories of Christ, e. g. Gospel of the Hebrews—Peter—the Egyptians—Marcion—All probably heretical corruptions of the 4 canonical gospels. All now lost.

§ 411. II. Supplementary Gospels—(1.) Of the infancy of Christ, e. g. (*a*) Protevangelium Jacobi Minoris—early history of Virgin—birth of Christ—comparatively simple and without exaggeration—Greek like that of the New Testament—Date very early—read at the festivals of Mary in the Eastern Church.

§ 412. (2.) Evangelium Nativitatis Mariæ—same general character—Latin preface by two bishops represents Matthew as the author—and Jerome as the translator. Collection of very old aprocryphal traditions.

§ 413. 3. Gospel of Joachim and Anna—parentage and birth of Virgin—infancy of Christ—flight to Egypt—infant miracles—Latin—purports to be by James. This also a collection of still older legends.

§ 414. 4. Gospel of Joseph the carpenter—Arabic translated from the Coptic—Life and death of Joseph—Moralizing—probably not older than the fourth century.

§ 415. 5. Gospel of Christ's infancy—Arabic translation from Syriac—full of absurd miracles. 6. Gospel of Thomas—Life of Christ from fifth to twelfth year—still more extravagant and silly.

§ 416. I. Supplementary accounts of his Passion, e. g. (1.) Gospel of Nicodemus—written in Greek—formal record of trial before Pilate—and resurrection of two sons of Simeon—dated in reign of Theodosius—first part purports to be derived from Hebrew work of Nicodemus—second part from older apocrypha—First mentioned in 13th century.

§ 417. (2.) Acts of Pilate—(*a*) such a book mentioned by Justin Martyr—Tertullian—Eusebius—Epiphanius—Pilate's report concerning Christ to Tiberius; with Tiberius's proposition to the Senate and letter to his mother—(*b*) Under Maximin—a heathen forgery—same title—blashpemous calumnies of Christ—read in schools by order of emperor—(*c*) A third book—same title—still extant—much later—Latin report of Pilate to Tiberius—with account of Pilate's punishment—also Epistle of Lentulus to Senate—with minute description of Christ's person—first mentioned in the Middle Ages.

§ 418. II. Apocryphal acts—mostly of gnostic origin—numerous in third and fourth centuries—13 in Tischendorf's collection—chiefly of the third century—some re-written with modification of gnosticism—all worthless—latest and largest—Historia Certaminis Apostolorum—purports to be written in Hebrew by Abdias, disciple of the Apostles and first Bishop of Babylon—Greek by Eutropius—and Latin by Julius Africanus—really not older than ninth century—found in the 16th century—rejected by Paul IV.—Baronius, Bellarmin, and Tillemont.

§ 419. III. Apocryphal Epistles—(*a*) Christ and Abgarus—King of Edessa—preserved in archives—seen there by Eusebius—request to be healed—promise to send disciple—(*b*) Paul to the Laodiceans (Col. 4, 16),—only in Latin—a mere cento of scriptural phrases—(*c*) Paul to the Corinthians (1 Cor. 5, 9), with their answer, both extant in Armenian—(*d*) Paul to Seneca—old tradition of correspondence (Augustine and Jerome)—13 short letters extant—(*e*) letter of Ignatius to Virgin Mary—asking information about Christ—and her answer referring him to John—first mentioned by Bernard in 12th century—(*f*) letters of the Virgin to the people of Messina, Florence, &c.

§ 420. IV. Apocryphal Apocalypses. (1.) Of Peter (Clem. Alex.) signs of judgment—(2.) Ascension of Paul (2 Cor. 12,) Aug. "fabulis plena stultissima præsumtione." Epiphanius says Cainite (3.) Thomas—(4.) Stephen—(5.) another of John—all wretched copies of canonical Apocalypse.

§ 421. V. Apocryphal prophecies. (1.) Old Testament. (*a*) Testament of the Twelve Patriarchs—Imitation of Gen. 49—Mysteries of the other world—Prophecies of Christ—rejection of Jews—fine style—mentioned by Origen—(*b*) Apocalypse of Moses—only two quotations in Syncellus—rejects circumcision—(*c*) Ascension of Isaiah—Imitations of Paul's conversation with Angel—Messianic Prophecies—Quoted by Origen, Epiphanius—Jerome—Greek lost—Latin version extant at Venice—Ethiopic at Oxford.

§ 422. (2.) Heathen prophecies—(*a*) Sibylline

books—Etymology of name (Σιὸς [Doric for Διὸς] Βουλή)—Varro quoted by Lactantius—Ten Sibyls —Chief at Cuma—Tarquin—3 books—burnt in Capitol—under Marius and Sylla (B. C. 183)—replaced by collection—burnt again under Nero (A. D. 64)—Sibylline books now extant—Homeric verse —by daughter-in-law of Noah—evidently by Christians—prophecies of Christ and Antichrist—Rome —Church—end of world—eruption of Vesuvius (A. D. 79)—sign of judgment—Nero's reappearance —Something later—gradual collection—second and third centuries—cited by Apologists—hence called Sibyllists—Celsus charged with forging—Disappeared with Paganism in fourth century—reappeared in 16th—only eight known till Mai discovered xi.–xiv.—best edition Alexandre's (1842)—(*b*) Hystaspes (Gushtasp) old Persian King—Christian prophecies—quoted by Justin Martyr and Clem. Alex.—(*c*) Hermes Trismegistus—Egyptian sage.

§ 423. IV. Disciplinary Pseudepigrapha—intended to give apostolical authority to ecclesiastical usages of third and fourth centuries—(1.) Apostolical polity or discipline—in Greek, third century—Acts of Apostolical Council—All exhort and legislate—Cephas besides Peter—also Martha and Mary —Part as old as beginning of second century?

§ 424. (2.) Apostolical Constitutions—eight books—duties of laity and clergy—worship—widows and deaconesses—treatment of poor—martyrs—festivals—heresies—Mosaic law—liturgy—charismata—ordinations—tythes—six books form one whole—called "Apostolic doctrine" in old versions—and in book itself—not ultra hierarchical—seventh and eighth each complete in itself—internal evidence of Syrian origin—last of third century—or beginning of fourth—Earlier than Council of Nice—quoted by Eusebius and Athanasius as "Doctrine of Apostles"—Cited as authority by Epiphanius—rejected by Concilium Quinisextum (692) as corrupted—but received in Eastern Church—unknown in West till 16th century—rejected by Baronius and Daillè—now generally given up.

§ 425. (3.) Apostolical Canons—Appendix to Constitutions (§ 424), but also in separate form—Greek—Syriac—Ethiopic—Arabic—Longer form 85 canons—shorter 50—peremptory tone—apostolical authority—not doctrinal but disciplinary—made known in West by Dionysius Exiguus (end of fifth century)—rejected as apocryphal by Pope Hormisdas—gradually current—recognized by Pseudo Isidore in East—imposed by Concilium Quinisextum.

§ 426. All this illustrates history of canon—

shows critical process—New Testament homogeneous—and superior—not only to apocrypha and pseudepigrapha—but to

§ 427. Apostolical Fathers—third connecting link—earliest uninspired Christian writers—contemporaries and disciples of Apostles; Mark and Luke excluded as inspired.

§ 428. Simplicity and piety—without inspiration—divine or human—Hence genuineness of extant writings questioned—because early disposition to claim apostolical origin for later usages and doctrines (§ 423)—no canon to prevent such frauds—not affecting rule of faith.

§ 429. But on the other hand—modern disposition to exaggerate critical misgivings—Too much expected from Apostolical Fathers—whereas great gulf—immense descent from Apostles to Apostolical Fathers.

§ 430. Guericke says this surprising only to Papists, who think successors no less inspired than Apostles, or to Rationalists, who think Apostles no more inspired than successors.

§ 431. Providential purpose of this inequality—to draw a broad line between the canon and all other writings. If Origen, Athanasius, or Augustin had immediately succeeded the Apostles—they might have rivalled them—but this prevented by a pause—during which the life of the Church was rather practical than intellectual.

§ 432. Collective edition of Cotelerius—recent one of Hefele. Translation by Archbishop Wake; number usually reckoned seven—three disciples of Paul—three of John—and one anonymous—Paul as Apostle of Gentiles—John as last survivor.

§ 433. I. School of Paul—all supposed to be named in his epistles.—1. Clemens Romanus (Phil. 4, 3)—early bishop—and martyr (Rufinus)—(*a*) Epistle to Corinthians—in Greek—exhortation to union and humility—read in churches—then lost sight of —1628—Codex Alexandrinus—with LXX. and New Testament—presented by Cyril Lucaris to Charles I.—(*b*) Same manuscript, fragment of second epistle to Corinthians—but no epistle—and probably not by Clement.—(*c*) Pseudepigrapha—(*d*) Apostolical Constitutions and Canons, (§§ 424, 425).—(*e*) Clementina and Recognitions.—(*f*) Some pseudodecretals.

§ 434. (2.) Barnabas—named in Galatians and Acts—one epistle extant—known to Clement of

Alexandria—lost since ninth century—found in 17th—first four and a half chapters only in old Latin version—allegorizes Old Testament—later than Fall of Jerusalem—depreciates ceremonial law—but pious—and some excellent ideas—reckoned apocryphal by Eusebius and Jerome (i. e. not inspired or canonical)—spurious by Neander—genuine by Gieseler.

§ 435. (3.) Hermas (Rom. 16, 14) "the Shepherd" complete only in old Latin version—Angel as Shepherd instructs Hermas—three books: I. Four visions (church as woman); + II. Twelve mandates (of Angel to Hermas); + III. Ten similitudes—Abstruse and mystical—but read in churches—Origen and Irenæus call it inspired—Muratori Fragment (Caius?) ascribes to another Hermas—brother of Pius, bishop of Rome (c. A. D. 150).

§ 436. II. School of John—belonging to his later ministry—age not mentioned in the Scriptures.—(1.) Ignatius—bishop of Antioch—martyred under Trajan (§ 490)—15 epistles extant, 8 acknowledged to be spurious (5 Greek + 3 Latin)—7 in Greek—written on way to Rome—1 to Polycarp—5 to churches in Asia Minor and 1 to church in Rome—warning against heresies and discord—exhortations to rally round the bishops as representatives of Christ—Hence appealed to in episcopal controversy—One question as to long and short recension.

whether long interpolated—or short curtailed. Third recension—discovered by Tatham (1838), edited by Cureton—glorified by Bunsen—refuted by Baur—only three epistles—in Syriac—less prelatical—but also less trinitarian—meagre garbling of the seven—Anglicans hold to long form—Germans to short—Inconclusive as to prelacy—(*a*) because bishop may mean presbyter—(*b*) if diocesan, a new invention.

§ 437. (2.) Polycarp—disciple of John—bishop of Smyrna—martyr under Marcus Aurelius (A. D. 168, § 494).—Epistles to churches under persecution—only one preserved—to the Philippians—Greek only in fragments—entire only in old Latin version—many citations from New Testament—important witness as to Canon.

§ 438. (3.) Papias, bishop of Hierapolis in Phrygia—disciple of John (Irenæus)—Martyr under Marcus Aurelius (?)—collector of Christ's *ΛΟΓΙΑ*—credulous and injudicious (*σμικρος νουν*, Eus.) but great influence—promoted Chiliasm—Only meagre fragments—preserved by Irenæus and Eusebius.

§ 439. III. Anonymous—Epistle to Diognetus—Description or Defence of Christianity—addressed to a heathen—Long ascribed to Justin Martyr—but very unlike—older—professed disciple of Apostles—more elegant—laxer as to Judaism—heathen gods nullities, not demons—First disproved by Tillemont—reaffirmed by Otto—(Excellent Patristic exercise—Hefele's edition (§ 432)—Biblical Repertory, Jan. 1853.

§ 440. Early propagation of Christianity—another connecting link with apostolical times—absolute and relative historical importance. New Testament, chiefly Peter and Paul.

§ 441. Remarkable dearth of information—almost a blank—perhaps to be explained by rapid and simultaneous movement—if slower and successive, might be traced more easily.

§ 442. Edessa—Christian king—Abgarus (170)—Arabia—India—Bartholomew?—Thomas?—Pautænus—Origen—Gaul from Asia Minor—Britain from the same?—or from Rome?—Eleutherus and Lucius—Claims of various nations mostly fabulous.

§ 443. Mode of propagation—as at first—by establishing radiating centres—Rome the last in the New Testament—then Alexandria and Carthage.

§ 444. Twofold conflict of the Church in the first centuries (§ 257)—Intellectual and physical—Intellectual conflict—(1) with avowed enemies—(2) with disguised enemies—A. Judaism (§ 391).

§ 445. B. Heathenism—(*a*) its origin—segregation of the chosen people—the rest left to walk in their own ways—(*b*) its tendencies to atheism and pantheism—to superstition—to materialism—to nature-worship—to despotism.

§ 446. Twofold preparation for Christianity, (1) among the Jews—salvation for men—(2) among the gentiles—men for salvation ; (*a*) negative—convince of need—and worthlessness of human contrivances—(*b*) positive—with actual cultivation—preparation of language—as the garb of truth—Greek—most perfect language—and when Christ came—the most prevalent—and therefore proper vehicle of œcumenical revelation.

§ 447. State of heathenism at the advent—effete—sense of want never greater—means of satisfying it never less.

§ 448. Barbarous religions, i. e. neither Greek nor Roman—comparativly little known—Eastern theosophies—Buddhism—Parsism—western Druidism—spiritual tyranny—power destroyed in first century. Other barbarous religions, military or savage.

§ 449. Greek and Roman Heathenism—originally not the same—the Roman sterner and purer—but assimilated after fall of Carthage and Corinth—increase of wealth and luxury—influence of Greek teachers—question as to Greek art—whether corrupting or redeeming (Tholuck and Jacobs).

§ 450. Sense of spiritual want unsatisfied—mania for new religions—fostered by new conquests—rites and mysteries imported from Egypt and the East—Dea Syra—Mithras—Syncretism—highest ranks—even Emperors—Heliogabalus—Alexander Severus. (§§ 500, 501).

§ 451. Relation of Philosophy to Mythology—(1) Antagonistic—condemned and ridiculed it—(2) Compromise—defended and explained it—symbolical interpretation—(3) Amalgamation—philosophy no longer speculation—but religion—especially after rise of Christianity.

§ 452. The greatest schools of Greek Philosophy extinct or metamorphosed, e. g. those of Plato and Aristotle still survived, and prevalent at Advent—those of (1) Epicurus—happiness the highest good—no Providence—the gods indifferent to man's conduct and condition— and (2) Zeno (Stoics) pain no evil—fate—indifferentism—apathy—No. 1 suited the Greeks—No. 2 the Romans. (See Acts 17, 18.)

§ 453. Heathen view of Christianity—at first contemptuous—as barbarous fanaticism—or offshoot of Judaism—then jealous—when it spread and became powerful—as new form of philosophy—all that was good in it known before—only in new form—But this led necessarily to

§ 454. Reform of Heathenism—(like that of Popery after the Reformation)—by reviving old systems—sp. that of Pythagoras—but no longer esoteric—popular—Goetes—Magoi—chief representative

§ 455. Apollonius of Tyana—lived through the first century—perhaps an enthusiast more than an impostor—oldest authorities speak of him as a Goes—but the next age exalted him as an antichrist—religious teacher and thaumaturge—sp. his biographer, Philostratus—but effect transient.

§ 456. Revival of old Mysteries—Eleusinian—Dionysian—Oriental—Egyptian—purer theology?—or mere freemasonry?—Still a failure—could not replace Christianity.

§ 457. Last effort—the *Eclectic Philosophy*—its

principle—take what is good in all systems—not only of philosophy—but of religion—thus sure to be better than any one—(a common fallacy—excels each only in detail—but has no unity or substantive existence; illustrate by eclectic building or machine)—Christianity itself placed under contribution—but not its essentials—then would have been Christian, and chiefly in heretical corrupted form.

§ 458. Basis of course not Christian—but Heathen Philosophy most like it—*Platonism*—hence *Neoplatonism*—supported by whole strength of Heathenism—in decline of classic age—Forerunners—*Plutarch* (+120)—profound—serious—sometimes almost Christian—favourite ancient with unlearned readers now—*Apuleius* (c. 170)—*Maximus Tyrius* (c. 190.)

§ 459. Proper founder of system—*Ammonius Saccas* of Alexandria (c. 243)—said to have been born and bred a Christian—seduced into heathenism by study of philosophy. Principal disciples and successors: Plotinus—also an Egyptian (c. 270)—Porphyry of Tyre (+ 304)—Jamblichus of Chalcis (+ 333)—witnessed fall of Heathenism.

§ 460. End of third century—universal among

educated heathen—superseded other systems—necessary part of education—studied by many Christians—led to some corruptions.

§ 461. Outline of system—two sets of gods—different spheres—mundane and extramundane—demons, good and bad—*κοσμος νοητος* or rational universe—material universe made by demiurge—*οἱ πολλοι* might be satisfied with local and ancestral gods—*οἱ σπουδαιοι* should seek to know and be united with *ὁ νοῦς* or *τὸ ἕν*—by ascesis—contemplation—and theurgy.

§ 462. Effect on Christianity—led many to it—others satisfied without it—some led to oppose it—early tone of heathen writers towards Christianity—Tacitus—Suetonius—Pliny—Marcus Aurelius—offended by enthusiasm. Of less note: Fronto—Crescens—Galen.

§ 463. Lucian—satirist of mythology—cynicism—and Christianity—promoted undesignedly by bearing witness to Christian fortitude and philadelphia.—His history of Peregrinus Proteus—aimed more at cynicism than at Christianity—founded in fact—(Peregrinus Proteus mentioned by A. Gellius—Tatian—Athenagoras—Tertullian)—but embellished fiction—with traits from Christian history —e. g. martyrdom of Polycarp.

§ 464. First formal attack on Christianity—by Celsus—probably Epicurean, with Platonic mark—*ΑΛΗΘΗΣ ΛΟΓΟΣ*—only known from Origen's refutation—some wit—but shallow—ignorant—malignant—makes Christ an ordinary Goes.

§ 465. *Porphyry* (§ 459)—nobler and abler—fifteen books (KATA CHRISTINIANΩN LOGOI) —only a few fragments in Eusebius—sceptical criticism—allegorical interpretation—contradictions —Moses and Christ—Peter and Paul—anachronisms—Daniel. Forerunner of rationalism—also wrote in defence of Heathenism ("Philosophy from the Oracles")—large fragments in Eusebius.

§ 466. *Hierocles*—governor of Bithynia under Diocletian—both persecutor and polemic writer—(*ΛΟΓΟΙΦΙΛΑΛΗΘΕΙΣΠΡΟΣΧΡΙΣΤΙΑΝΟΥΣ*) —best part borrowed from predecessors—eked out with calumnious fables about Christ and Christians —prefers Apollonius of Tyana.

§ 467. These attacks called forth the best Christian writers of the age—sp. under Antonines—in Apologies—or regular defences of Christianity—some public or official—some popular or private.

Of both these some are lost—and some still extant.

§ 468. Oldest apologists no longer extant—(1) Quadratus—disciple of Apostles (Irenæus)—Bishop of Athens (Eusebius)—reputed prophet—had seen men healed or raised to life by Christ—presented Apology to Adrian—lost since the seventh century—last mentioned by Photius—(2) Ariston of Pella—"Jason and Papiscus"—argument from prophecy—sneered at by Celsus—defended by Origen.

§ 469. (3) *Melito of Sardis*—witness to Canon—presented apology to Marcus Aurelius—praised by Eusebius and Jerome—original lost—Syriac version found and published with an English translation in 1855, by Cureton. (4) *Claudius Apollinaris*—bishop of Hierapolis—praised by Eusebius and Jerome—now lost. (5) *Miltiades*—a rhetorician—presented apology to Marcus Aurelius—praised by Eusebius and Jerome—now lost.

§ 470. II. Apologists still extant: (1) Justin Martyr—born at Shechem in Samaria—heathen parentage and education—studied philosophy—tried all schools—but unsatisfied—at last instructed by an aged Christian—retained his philosopher's mantle—but travelled as a sort of missionary—

hated by the heathen—put to death at Rome (163–167)—at the instance of Crescens the Cynic (§ 462.)

§ 471. Two Apologies of Justin—first and longest to Antoninus Pius—second to Marcus Aurelius—a third against the Jews (Dialogue with Trypho)—Against the heathen *ΠΕΡΙ ΜΟΝΑΡ-ΧΙΑΣ*)—refuted from their own philosophers. Some books of doubtful origin—two Exhortations to the Greeks. Book against heresies now lost—many pseudopigrapha—e. g. Epistle to Diognetus (§ 439).

§ 472. *Tatian*—disciple of Justin—author of first harmony (Diatessaron)—*ΛΟΓΟΣΠΡΟΣ* HEL-LENAS—treats Greek heathenism with indiscriminate contempt. Afterwards became a Gnostic.

§ 473. (3.) *Athenagoras*—personal history unknown—*Presbeia* (intercession) *peri Christianôn*—clear and logical—negative and positive defence—another work defends the resurrection against heathen objections.—(4) *Theophilus of Antioch*—three books to Antolycus—a learned heathen friend—among the best apologies—shows great knowledge of Greek literature. Born a heathen—converted by reading the Scriptures—author of other exegetical and controversial works—now lost. (5) *Hermias*—history unknown—*ΔΙΑΣΥΡΜΟΣ ΤΩΝ ΕΞΩ ΦΙΛΟΣΟΦΩΝ*—satirical attack on heathenism—variously described as "geistvoll" (Kurtz) and "geistlos" (Jacobi). [Tertullian, Origen, Minucius Felix?]

§ 474. General character of these Apologies—repel calumnies—atheism, misanthrophy—Thyesean feasts—incest—show the true character of Christianity—and expose the absurdity and wickedness of heathenism—thus they dispelled many errors and prejudices—and diffused much light—both as to Heathenism and Christianity.

§ 475. But good end frequently promoted by bad means—e. g. (*a*) appeal to false authorities—Sibylline books—Hystaspes—Hermes Trismegistus—(*b*) identifying Christianity with the old Greek philosophy—(*c*) erroneous views of the relation between Judaism and Christianity—depreciation of the Ceremonial law—even as a temporary institution—(*d*) deficient views of spiritual Christianity—too superficial and external.

§ 476. Other side of great twofold conflict (§ 444). Persecution—coextensive with first three centuries.—Providential purpose or final cause—1. To sift the Church and exclude hypocritical professors. 2. To harden and fortify it by endurance.

Peculiarly necessary in the first age, as the forming period of the Church.

§ 477. Primary source of Persecution—the Jews —begins in New Testament—Persecution of Christ by the Pharisees—as the dominant party—which he especially denounced—and of the Apostles by the Sadducees—because they preached the resurrection.

§ 478. The first martyr, Stephen—the second, James, the son of Zebedee—both led to the diffusion of the gospel—Persecution by Saul and of Paul (active and passive)—Jewish hatred embittered by the death of Christ—the Zealots.

§ 479. First check to Jewish persecution—the destruction of Jerusalem by Titus (§ 387). Renewed under Bar Cochba (or Bar Coziba)—aided by Rabbi Akiba—insurrection—three years war—Christians persecuted by both parties—put down by Julius Severus—Palestine wasted—Jerusalem razed—Roman colony—Ælia Capitolina —temple of Venus—Jews banished for ages (Tert. and Jerome)—Circumcision and Sabbath forbidden —end of Jewish persecution.

§ 480. Secondary source of Persecution—Heathenism—necessary hostility to exclusive religion—

law of Ten Tables—only one religio licita—i. e. in Rome and Italy—tolerated religion of foreign conquests.

§ 481. Less tolerant to Judaism—because exclusive—still less to Christianity—because more aggressive and successful—and without prestige of nationality and antiquity—(compare Turkish and Prussian toleration).

§ 482. Popular prejudice against the Chrstians —(*a*) as Atheists—because no images or temples—(*b*) as licentious—on account of secret and nocturnal meetings—Lord's Supper a Thyestean feast!—(*c*) as unpatriotic—because declined civil and military service—not as unlawful *per se*—but as leading to idolatry—(*d*) as misanthropical—because abstained from public amusements—and thought more of the future than the present.

§ 483. Promoted by mutual abuse of church and sects—and influence of Priests—and other interested parties—fomenting popular illusions—as to public calamities—anger of gods for desecration —Tertullian: "Deus non pluit, duc ad Christianos!"—"Si Tiberis ascendit in mænia, si Nilus non ascendit in arva—si cœlum stetit—si terra movet—si fames, si lues, statim, Christianos ad leonem!"

§ 484. Common to government and people—fear of political ascendancy—chiliastic dreams—fall of empire—or real doctrine of Messiah's kingdom—submissive citizens but dangerous.

§ 485. Guericke's classification of Persecutions (1) governmental—(2) popular—(3) individual—Kurtz's: (1) Chronological division to Trajan—(2) to Marcus Aurelius—(3) to Philip the Arabian—(4) under Decius—(5) under Diocletian.

§ 486. Persecutions of first century—Early Emperors—Tiberius—afraid to persecute—wicked but superstitious—conscience-stricken—traditional proposition to deify Christ (Tertullian)—Claudius expelled Jews (Acts xviii.)—and Christians with them?—(Quote Suetonius.)—As yet not distinguished from the Jews.

§ 487. First real persecution—under Nero—conflagration—wanton cruelty—false accusation—related by Tacitus and Suetonius—("per flagitia invisos" .... "exitiabilis superstitio" .... "odio humani generis convicti.")—General or local—former asserted first by Orosius (§ 88). Spanish inscription to Nero.—First decree against Christianity? (Tertullian says, other Neronic laws repealed). Perhaps meant to be general—but not executed.

§ 488. Successors of Nero spared the church—until Domitian—political jealousy—Flavius Clemens—Flavia Domitilla banished to Pontia—John to Patmos—boiling oil (Tertullian)—date of Apocalypse—two of Christ's kinsmen—heirs of David (Hegesippus ap. Eusebius)—Temporary respite under Nerva.

§ 489. New era in history of Persecution—reign of Trajan—not from personal hostility—but policy—revived laws against secret societies—(Blunt says Nero's edict against Christianity). Correspondence with Pliny—no general rule—no inquisition—no anonymous charges—but if obstinate, to die—(genuineness of correspondence denied by Gibbon and Semler—still disputed—but commonly received).—First regular law of persecution (Blunt says Nero's)—but no heathen bigotry or fanatical zeal ("pessimi exempli nec nostri seculi.")—Old Roman spirit—indifferent till conflict with civil authority—then inflexibly severe.

§ 490. Extent of Persecution—certainly to Palestine and Syria—Symeon, son of Clopas—nephew of Joseph (Hegesippus)—Bishop of Jerusalem—arraigned—as Christian and Davidite—scourged—crucified (A. D. 107).—Antioch—Ignatius—audience of Emperor—sent in chains to Rome—(wrote seven epistles on the way. § 436)—exposed in Coliseum to wild beasts—(A. D. 107–116.)

§ 491. Hadrian—zealous heathen—but forbade extra-judicial persecution—and tumultuary accusation—tradition of fourth century—built first churches—knew little of Christianity—cared less—profaned Jerusalem—report from Serenius Granianus, Proconsul of Asia Minor—instructions to his successor, Minucius Fundanus.

§ 492. Antoninus Pius—mild and benevolent—tried to quell persecution [Melito]—but people excited by calamities—rescript ad commune Asiæ—preserved by Eusebius—but now thought spurious.

§ 493. Thus far political—not personal hostility—till Marcus Aurelius—most pious of heathen—yet hated Christianity—stoical contempt of its enthusiasm and condescension (§ 462)—irrational and obstinate fanaticism—resolved to suppress it—not merely passive but active—espionage and torture—Extant edict—genuine (Neander)?—or spurious

(Gieseler)?—Law of Marcus Aurelius in Pandects —punishing "religious superstition" with deportation.

§ 494. Persecution general but not uniform—at Rome—Justin (165–168)—instigated by Crescens (§§ 462, 470.)—Worst in Asia Minor and Gaul—contemporary accounts (§ 80)—Smyrna—Polycarp—aet. 86 (§ 442)—disciple of John—Lyons and Vienne—Pothinus aet. 90—Ponticus aet. 15—slave Blandina—ashes in Rhone.

§ 495. Old tradition of Legio Fulminea (or Fulminatrix)—A. D. 174.—War with Quadi and Marcomanni—drought—storm—prayers of Christians—end of persecution (Claudius Apollinaris and Tertullian)—but anachronism—and heathen version—Jupiter Pluvius—Egyptian sorcerer.

§ 496. Successors of Marcus personally indifferent—but persecuting laws unrepealed—at mercy of local governors—Commodus—Marcia—local persecutions—Asia Minor—Arrius Pontinus Proconsul (Tertullian)—Did the Emperor himself turn?

§ 497. Septimius Severus—healed by Proculus, a Christian slave—anointed (James 5, 14)—hence favoured Christianity at first (Tertullian)—but afterwards turned—cause unknown—Montanistic extravagance and prophecies of Christ's personal reign? Edict forbidding gentiles, Judæos, or Christianos fieri (A. D. 203).

§ 498. Persecution raged in Egypt and Northwest Africa—Alexandria—Leonidas—father of Origen beheaded—Potamiena and her mother Marcella—Saturnus ("know me at the judgment")—Perpetua of Carthage—slave Felicitas—contemporary record—with extracts from Jail Journal.

§ 499. Caracalla—misanthropic indifference—but persecution still continued—new practice of purchasing exemption—disapproved by earnest Christians. (Tertullian de Fuga in Persecutione.)

§ 500. Syncretistic mania (§ 450). Heliogabalus priest of sun—wished to unite all religions in one ritual and temple—hence tolerated all—Christianity included—(compare James II.)

§ 501. *Alexander Severus* (222)—more rational eclecticism—(anecdote—any religion better than a tavern)—appreciated spiritual worship—bust of Christ in his Lararium—with those of Abraham, Orpheus, and Apollonius—recognized church at Rome as legal corporation—influenced by his mother, Julia Mammæa—and she by Origen—(Orosius says she was a Christian—Eusebius says, pious, if ever a woman was)—golden rule on wall of palace—hence reputed Jew or Christian—nicknamed Archienus and Archisynagogus.

§ 502. *Maximin the Thracian* (235)—murdered and succeeded Alexander—hated Christians for his sake—persecuted chief men—as his own opponents—earthquakes excited popular rage—reign too short to do much harm.

§ 503. *Gordian* (244)—left the Christians unmolested—*Philip the Arabian*—so tolerant—afterwards said to be a Christian—and called first Christian emperor by Jerome—and to have been disciplined by a bishop. (Eusebius as a tradition—Jerome as a fact.) He and Queen (Severa) also friends of Origen (§ 501.)—Origen against Celsus (§ 464) says persecution at an end—but to be renewed.

§ 504. Pauses between persecutions—intervals of rest and growth—increase of strength and numbers—heightened expectations of ascendency—increased opposition—and prepared for new attack.

§ 505. Decian persecution—the most methodical—extensive—inquisitorial—and cruel—hitherto the martyrs were few and easily numbered—(Origen.) Now fell chiefly on bishops and clergy—but all required to sacrifice—flight allowed but not return—confiscation of goods—many fled to desert—first anchorites—Paul of Thebes.

§ 506. Church weakened by repose—increase of apostates—Lapsi—classification. The 3 classes of the lapsed were: (1.) Sacrificati. (2.) Thurificati. (3.) Libellatici—certificates of sacrifice registered as heathen—condemned by zealous Christians —("nefandus idololatriæ libellus"—Cyprian cf. § 499)—Proportionate zeal and steadfastness of confessors—Legend of Seven Sleepers—Gregory of Tours—awoke under Theodosius II. (447) and saw the cross everywhere.

§ 507. Death of Decius (251) seemed to lay storm—but people roused by plague and famine—Gallus urged to persecute—would if could—but hindered by political commotions—and soon died.

§ 508. *Valerian* (253)—at first favourable—but when Christianity spread in higher ranks—listened to his favourite *Macrian*—banished ministers—forbade meetings—next year began to slay ministers and chief laymen—so that Christians thought Rev. 13, 5 fulfilled.—(Dionysius Alexandrinus apud Eusebius).

§ 509. Martyrs at Rome: Bishop *Sixtus*—and four deacons—one of them St. *Lawrence*—broiled alive. At Carthage: *Cyprian*—Christian courtiers now degraded—Acta—and life by Pontius—next year Persian war—death and captivity of Valerian—narrow escape of Church.

§ 510. *Gallienus* spared Christians—perhaps from indolence—but not merely negative—important positive measure—beginning of end—two decrees preserved by Eusebius—Christianity recognized as *religio licita* (259).

§ 511. *Aurelian*—zealous heathen—but just and politic—long spared Christianity—restrained by decree of Gallienus—and occupied with military enterprises—at last digested plan of persecution—but execution prevented by military conspiracy—and death.

§ 512. Another interval—long pause in storm of persecution—seemed to be abandoned—Christianity allowed to spread for many years—but only preparation for the last and worst.

§ 513. Diocletian—(284)—zealous heathen—but good-natured—and cautious—afraid of Christians—respected act of Gallienus—wife and daughter Christians—but favourite scheme to restore empire—and with it the old religion—new organization—two Augusti and two Cesars.

§ 514. Maximian—Augustus of the West—persecutor before—Legend of the Theban legion—much embellished—simplest account—seventy Christian soldiers refused to march against their brethren and were massacred with their commander Mauritius—at St. Maurice.

§ 515. Galerius—son-in-law of Diocletian—and Cesar—bigoted and fanatical heathen—leader of that party—unwearied in conjunction with Maximian—A. D. 298, purged army of Christians.

§ 516. A. D. 303. Meeting of Emperors at Nicomedia—consulted gods and men—Christian church there pulled down—next day—decree—closing churches—burning books—new class of apostates—*Traditores* (i. e. librorum sacrorum)—subterfuge—substituted other books—Christians excluded from office—Christian slaves from hope of freedom—edict pulled down—palace fired—charged on Christians.

§ 517. Four more edicts—prisons soon filled—height of persecution 304—sacrifice or die—almost whole empire—wonders of heroism and cowardice—but fewer lapsed than under Decius—new torments—beasts revolted (Eusebius). Sanguine hopes—monuments to commemorate extirpation of Christianity.

§ 518. Diocletian and Maximian abdicated (305)—Galerius and Constantius Chlorus succeeded—Constantius Chlorus had spared the Christians as much as possible—in Spain—Gaul—and Britain—Maximin continued persecution in the East—exclude from cities—forbade church-building—circulated forged Acts of Pilate—caused to be read in schools—sprinkled food in market with sacrificial wine.

§ 519. Galerius on death-bed—conscience-stricken—or hope of restoration by Christian God—first edict (311)—still extant—had tried to restore Christians, who had left *parentum suorum sectam*—but in vain—" quamplurimi perseverant "—" indulgentiam credidimus porrigendam"—better be Christians than nothing—" ut denuo sint Christiani et *conventicula* sua componant "—provided nothing " contra disciplinam "—and pray to their God for us and the republic—that they may lead quiet lives.

§ 520. Constantine—son of Constantius Chlorus—same dispositions—proclaimed by army in Britain—opposed by Maxentius in Italy and Africa—ignoble bigot—turned against Christians because favoured by Constantine. On march against Maxentius—Constantine saw cross in sky—various versions—certainly put cross in hand of statue—and adopted labarum (doubtful etymology). Conquers Maxentius—Licinius in Illyricum—312 edict tolerating all religions misunderstood—313 edict of Milan—allowing free profession of Christianity—Maximin submits—and dies soon—Licinius quarrels with Constantine and heads heathen party—war of life and death—Constantine conquers—end of persecution (323–4).

§ 521. Ten Persecutions—old reckoning—founded on Plagues of Egypt?—or Rev. 17, 12–14?—or mere coincidence—Two accounts—Sulpicius Severus—Historia Sacra (2, 33)—ten plagues predicted—nine past—that of Antichrist to come. Augustine (Civ. Dei. 18, 52)—"nonnullis visum est vel videtur"—no more persecution until Antichrist—but he thinks only ingenious conjecture—without inspired authority.

§ 522. 1. Nero. 2. Domitian. 3. Trajan.
4. { M. Aurelius A / Adrian S } 5. { S. Severus A / Mamilius S }
6. { Maximin A / Severus S } 7. Decius. 8. Valerian.
9. { Aurelian A / Diocletian S } 10. Diocletian A.

§ 523. Question as to severity of persecutions—

and number of martyrs—modern disposition to extenuate—Dodwell—Semler—Hase—partly reaction from old exaggerations (e. g. St. Ursula and eleven thousand virgins—martyred on pilgrimage under Maximin (§ 502)—said to be mistake of tombstone—XIM(artyres) for XI (mille) partly from confounding earlier and later periods—few martyrs before Origen (§ 509.)

§ 524. Some from wrong motives—shame—vanity—sympathy—fear—fanaticism—insanity. Still "noble army of martyrs"—old Greek and Roman heroism matched by Christian martyrs.

§ 525. Good effects of persecution—providential purpose answered (§ 476), but not perfectly—hypocrites and cowards after all.

§ 526. Positive bad effects—false notion of necessity and merit—false standard of duty—undue attention to mere suffering—with some the whole of religion (like temperance—antislavery—antipopery—millenarianism—charity—now)—false position of martyrs and confessors—led to early controversy—and first schisms.

www.ingramcontent.com/pod-product-compliance
Lightning Source LLC
LaVergne TN
LVHW020211110826
845151LV00003B/672

* 9 7 8 1 4 2 5 5 3 4 4 6 2 *